THEORY OF WAR AND PEACE. IMPERATIVES OF TIME. RUSSIA? UKRAINE? REASONS.

DIMITAR BANTUTOV

CONTENTS

AN OPEN LETTER TO ELON MUSK

I am writing this open letter to Elon Musk, and others like him who have billions, tens of billions, or hundreds of billions of dollars. These are people who possess vast wealth, wield considerable power, and are the financial elite of the modern world. I am addressing these individuals because I am convinced that right now, they can help the human race that inhabits planet Earth.

Russia and Ukraine are at war!

All of humanity is witnessing the war between Russia and Ukraine. No one imagined that at the beginning of the twenty-first century, humanity would witness a war fought between two Slavic peoples, between two countries that were communist in the twentieth century.

Just a few years ago, if someone had said that this was possible, they would have declared him insane, and they would have told him that what he was saying was nonsense. But as we see, the war happened. And what is most important, it happened in such a way that Russia and America put their nuclear weapons on combat alert. I have the feeling that at any moment, a nuclear conflict could begin. I am convinced that many more people on our planet think the same way.

All sane men, women and children know that if a nuclear war starts, it will be the last. After it, there will be no more wars, because there will be no living people.

People like me will die immediately. It will happen very easily. For example, I and a few billion other living human beings will go to sleep tonight, and the next morning, we will not wake up. We will not wake up because we will be dead. But that means we will die so quickly that we will be happy dead. And that's it. End of humanity.

Actually, I'm wrong, because there will still be people alive. For example, you Elon Musk will still be alive. You, and others like you, will still be alive. Because most likely, you have some very deep bunker, so deep that it's close to hell, and there you will be able to hide from the falling bombs.

Oh no! I remembered! You have an artificial satellite on Earth, and you will be able to climb very high, very close to heaven, and in this way you will still be saved from death. Yes, however, you probably feel that this will not solve your problem. You will be alive, but you will not feel well. Believe me, you will really suffer. This is because when I and many others like me are no longer on this planet, it will mean that your billions are no longer billions. What you have in the form of paper dollars will now be just ordinary paper. This is because dollars have value only when I, and others like me, are alive. In fact, during this war, you will suddenly lose all your money. You will be terribly poor. This is extremely unpleasant, isn't it?

The second danger that lurks for you is that you will be left alone. In fact, the truth is that you will not be completely alone. There will be a hundred more like you, or even a thousand, very rich, who are either in very deep holes underground, near hell, or very high up on artificial satellites, near heaven, where, in both cases, you will be alive. You will be alive, but believe me, you will not be happy. All day long you will think and remember what planet Earth was like before the bombs fell, when I and others like me were still alive. You will dream of sunrises and sunsets, rivers, seas, blue oceans and green forests and many other wonderful things that no longer exist. And you should know that you will be unhappy. The most ordinary, miserable miserable. You will be unhappy because you are social beings. Because homo sapiens inhabiting this planet has historically evolved as a social being. This is extremely important, but the majority of people inhabiting our planet are not aware of this fact. There are psychologists and psychiatrists who have done special theoretical analyses, as a result of which the conclusion is that if a social individual, in this case homosapiens, is left alone in the Universe, he will very quickly make a categorical decision that he must burst his skull. You understand, he will decide to commit suicide. The only reason for this decision is that he is a social individual, and precisely for this reason, without others like him, he cannot continue his existence. This is a fundamental principle that operates in the entire Reality. This principle is written at the base of the quantum wave matrix, of the One Infinite Reality. You probably know that as a state of energy, this matrix is located behind the Planck quantum, and the information that is written there represents laws that are of the rank of Principles and Absolute Constants.

One of these principles states: Reason, always and everywhere, is social.

In other words, reason can be happy only when there are a sufficiently large number of people around it, those like it, who are of its kind and possess reason.

So Elon Musk, you and those like you, with a lot of money, will probably have to take care of your happy life, and your money. Because, happiness without money, that's real misery. Right?

Okay, what should be done?

It's easy! You and those like you must take care of the peace of our planet. To take care that there is no nuclear war on this planet. To take care that there are no nuclear weapons on this planet. In my opinion, this is the most important and greatest task facing all of you, the rich and super-rich, who inhabit planet Earth. This is a real challenge for you, and for others like you. But, you should know that a large part of the people on this planet do not believe that you will take on this task. A typical example in this regard was my father. A colonel, a professor, a doctor of philosophy, a staunch communist, of the old school, he was completely convinced that the representatives of the human race, who have a huge amount of money, and whom he called capitalists, would never spend any money to eliminate nuclear weapons. I do not agree with this opinion of his. Unlike him, I am convinced that there are rich people who want the elimination of nuclear weapons.

My father and I argued and argued and finally made a bet of five dollars. I suggest you help me win this bet. If I win, I promise we'll split it equally! The bets are two and a half dollars per person. It's not much, but it's money. Right?

A specific question arises:

What should be done to eliminate the nuclear threat from the face of planet Earth? This is a complex question, and it is subject to discussion. Most likely, many solutions can be proposed. And these solutions can be proposed by different people. Even by people like me, because I live on planet Earth, together with you.

I have a suggestion:

An agency must be created on our planet.

Agency for Nuclear Disarmament .

The short name of this institution will be THE AGENCY.

The AGENCY has one single goal: nuclear disarmament.

The AGENCY must be independent. This is the most important condition for it to function and fulfill its sole task. To be independent, this agency must be funded from sources that are independent.

Who are these sources Elon Musk? The answer is very short and clear. The funding of the AGENCY should be with the money of the richest people on this planet. People like you, and others like you, who have billions, tens of billions, hundreds of billions. You have to part with some of your money to fund this institution.

The AGENCY must be supranational.

The AGENCY must be supra-continental.

AGENCY must be above social.

The AGENCY must be above class.

AGENCY must be above race.

AGENCY must be above gender.

The AGENCY must be above political.

The AGENCY must be over the age of majority.

The AGENCY must be supra-ethnic.

And when we add up all these "over", "over", "over", what do we get?

Once again, it turns out that the only way for the AGENCY to be so many times "above" is to be financed from independent sources. This is possible only when this money is set aside by the people who own this money, and the owners can dispose of it individually, according to their own conscience, according to their own free will. These are people who can make decisions independently, without taking into account politics, economics, parties, classes, governments and any other such... I will not list. These are the people who, through their common, coordinated decisions, will in practice manage the AGENCY.

And one more thing. This is the only way that all of you rich and super rich can enter human history, and stay there forever.

Nuclear disarmament will be a long and difficult process. It will last for decades, and will encompass the entire Solar System. In time, the perimeter of the AGENCY's action will inevitably be expanded beyond the Solar System.

The AGENCY will use peaceful means to propagate the ideas of nuclear disarmament.

The AGENCY will hire experts to assess the nuclear threat at various points in the One Infinite Reality.

The AGENCY will convene forums to discuss the possibilities and methods for nuclear disarmament.

The AGENCY will research and develop new forms and methods for the removal and deactivation of nuclear weapons.

I stop listing, but I am clearly aware that more specific actions can be listed that aim at nuclear disarmament, of planet Earth, of the Solar System, of the One Infinite Reality.

I am convinced that this is exactly what has always been and always will be, the sole, fundamental mission of REASON. Not just the human one. I say this because we all know that there is also the non-human one.

An important question arises: where will the AGENCY be located?

I have a suggestion:

The AGENCY should be located on the territory of the Republic of Bulgaria. What considerations do I have when proposing this?

First.

The Republic of Bulgaria is the first Slavic, Orthodox, Cyrillic-writing state to be a member of NATO. This can be interpreted in two ways: NATO has managed to penetrate an Orthodox, Slavic, Cyrillic-writing state for the first time in its history. But this fact can also be viewed the other way around: Bulgaria is the first Orthodox Slavic, Cyrillic-writing state to penetrate NATO structures. This is an interesting fact that has significance.

Second.

The Republic of Bulgaria is in an extremely suitable place for the location of the AGENCY on its territory. Bulgaria is located at one of the largest, perhaps the largest, crossroads of peoples, interests, ethnicities, and cultures, starting from ancient times and up to the present. One of the most ancient civilizations on planet Earth has appeared on the territory of Bulgaria. Perhaps the most ancient. Let me remind you that the oldest gold treasure on Earth was found in Bulgaria. It is called the Varna Gold Treasure. It was made almost seven thousand years before the new era. I know how it happened. My great, great..... great grandfather made gold jewelry for my great grandmother, and then gave them to her. She was very happy, and immediately gifted him with many heirs. Now you know how the most ancient gold treasure was made, and

I hope you still have some sense of humor.

The territory of Bulgaria is the geographical point through which extremely important roads pass, from Asia to Europe, and from Europe to Asia and Africa. This is of great importance.

Third

The Bulgarian people are a very wise people, and I am convinced that they will welcome with open arms and joy the creation of such an institution on their territory.

Bulgarians know how to value important things, and especially the lives of other peoples and nationalities. As an example, I can cite the saving of the lives of Bulgarian Jews during World War II. Bulgarians will be able to protect the AGENCY from its enemies. Naturally, this protection will be possible only through the active help of other peoples, perhaps all who inhabit the Earth. I say this because I know that the AGENCY will need protection. I know that the AGENCY will have many, and very different enemies. Terribly many and terribly strong enemies. It has always been so, and it will always be so, because according to science, dialectics, the development of things, inevitably proceeds in this way, and obeys the laws of dialectical logic.

The third law of dialectics is: "The law of unity and struggle of opposites." It was defined by Hegel. In short, there will always be enemies, because that is how it should be, and that is normal.

I understand very well that the idea of creating an Agency for Nuclear Disarmament is in a very crude form, but so what. The important thing is that the idea is already alive, and it must be considered, because it is a question of the survival of humanity.

What would you say, Elon Musk? You and others like you. What would you all say? I think the idea is worth it. Think about it. It is necessary, because at this very moment, a terrible question is posed before all of humanity:

"To be or not to be?"

Evgeni Bantutov.

DIMITAR BANTUTOV

ebantutov @ mail . bg

REFLECTIONS

There is a war going on on Earth. Continuously.

Humanity dreams of Peace. Continuously.

These are facts. The reasons are terrible and ugly.

All Miss Worlds, in the end, want eternal peace. The people across the street are shiny. They clap and smile sweetly. Then they go to work. To produce weapons. This is shockingly funny.

Someone needs to explain...

Why is there war?

Why is there no eternal peace?

War and causes?

War and psychology?

Aggression and peace?

Crazy homo sapiens?

Are crazy people born or made?

Someone needs to explain...

EPIGRAPH.

"Politics is a mask. The mask hides greed for money and a thirst for power."

Dimitar Bantutov.

"Relative truth is always a lie. Political truth is always relative."

Evgeni Bantutov.

BISMARCK WROTE.

In 1870, Bismarck wrote:

"Russia's power can only be undermined by the separation of Ukraine...

It is necessary to incite two parts of one people and watch how brother kills brother. It is only necessary to find and raise traitors, and with their help to change the self-consciousness of the people to such an extent that they will hate everything Russian, to hate their own kind. Everything else is a matter of time. "

PROLOGUE

In 1986, Professor, Doctor of Philosophy, Colonel, Dimitar Petrov Bantutov, wrote a text that is not present in the 1990 book because the editor-in-chief removed the written text:

"The philosophical and methodological point of view allows us to admit and subject to dialectical analysis the idea that socialism as a socio-economic system has lost the battle with capitalism and has disappeared from the face of the planet Earth. Does this mean that the threat of nuclear apocalypse will automatically disappear and the nuclear arsenal will be buried for "eternal times", since the threat of the "mortal enemy" called socialism no longer exists?!

No! This is a deadly dangerous utopia, because in the "soul" of capitalism "a demonic force rages", for supremacy, for power, for large and super-large profits, for the conquest of neighboring peoples, for the appropriation of new territories, for the exploitation of new natural wealth and resources, for the satisfaction of all imperial ambitions, which is imperialism in its complete form, which leads to militarism in its complete form, which leads to the creation of ever more perfect, more efficient conventional and nuclear weapons, with the sole purpose, faster and cheaper, of taking human life. New historical realities direct the modern historical process, from the formula "who kills whom" to the diametrically opposite principle, to learn the great art of "living together", which means that peace between peoples and social systems is also becoming one of the imperatives of the time, and in all likelihood for a very long historical period."

In 1986, Dimitar Bantutov wrote that communism could disappear!?

In 1986, Dimitar Bantutov prophesied that there would be war!?

These ideas were in sharp contradiction with the official socialist doctrine. The totalitarian regime in Bulgaria persecuted the authors of such opinions. Dimitar Bantutov was disciplinary dismissed from the Military Academy G.S. Rakovski, was expelled from the ranks of the Bulgarian Communist Party, a procedure for dismissal was initiated, a procedure for revoking the rank of colonel, and a procedure for bringing him to judicial responsibility before a Military Court.

According to the words of the first democratically elected president of Bulgaria, Zhelyu Zhelev, Dimitar Bantutov is the only senior political officer who was actually repressed by the totalitarian regime in Bulgaria.

FOREWORD BY DIMITAR BANTUTOV.

In the distant past, the boundary that divided the unified human history of the Old and New Eras is lost. The world clock begins to count down the last decade, after which comes not only the twenty-first century, but also the third millennium. What boundary will be drawn here at this historical turning point? And right now the question arises: Is doom really the only fate of civilization?

One might think that the colossal and in many ways dramatic experience of the past millennia is enough for humanity to make sense of its past, present and future, in the spirit of reason and wisdom. After all, it is said that history is the best teacher of nations, right?

Unfortunately, however, the picture of the modern era is far from reasonable and even less wise, although history is indeed very instructive, if there is someone to listen to it. Having penetrated deep into the depths of nature, man turned out to be far from the secrets of its essence. The huge difference between the mastered forces of nature and the unmastered own essential forces has faced the entire human race with the terrible question: To be or not to be? And perhaps the saddest thing in this story is the cheerful way in which it is unfolding! Humanity should finally reach out with its hands and stop the action of those sinister levers of modern history, which can direct its existence to the freezing depths of eternal non-existence. To reach out, and with united efforts, to set all the hands of the World Clock to the division " **survival** ". However, this is still not noticed, and perhaps those authors are right who believe that the frivolity of modern civilization towards its own destiny is the most inexplicable phenomenon of modern history. Before the silent gaze of all humanity, a continuous chain of great confrontations continues to rage, giving history a spontaneous and uncontrollable character. Above all stands the unprecedented danger of a universal nuclear guillotine, and next to it is the specter of the ecological crisis creeping across the planet! The gap and distance between developed and underdeveloped countries and peoples is becoming deeper and deeper, and in many respects the only thing between them is reduced to the fact that they exist. They exist in the same physical time, but in fact the colossal difference between them turns them into almost peoples and people from completely different worlds. In a state of great opposition are: wealth versus poverty, good versus evil, the light of science versus the demonic power of ignorance, universal alienation versus disillusioned humanism, and culture versus pseudoculture.

Sometimes, the modern era is characterized as the last ascent of the most dangerous historical peak, something like the Everest of history, others prefer the even darker comparison with the final path, from the religious legend of the hill of Golgotha. Whatever comparison is accepted or rejected, whatever point of view is defended pessimistically or optimistically, there is only one situation that undoubtedly remains - at the end of the second millennium AD, history reaches such a critical limit where homo sapiens, not one but many silent sphinxes created by himself, stood before him, with the threatening question: "Either get to know us, or we will destroy you?!"

What the strategy of humanity will be from now on is difficult to predict, but its chance is increasingly linked to its ability to face the challenges of time as a unified force on the planet, that is, as the human race. Let us call this the strategy of the Great Alternative. And let us hope that it will become the banner of the transition to the twenty-first century and the third millennium. But, in order for this desire to become a reality, it is necessary to put an end to the sinister notion that someone is on earth by God's will, and someone else ended up here, completely by chance.

A new attitude is needed towards the common interests of all nations and people inhabiting our planet, because the millennial tradition in which the progress and well-being of some nations and individuals came at the expense of the misfortunes and troubles of others, and from which all modern monsters crawled out, has only one solution: this tradition must cease its action! Otherwise, the economic fall that lies at the bottom of this tradition will feed its monsters for the last time, and the price will be all of humanity.

1. THE PHILOSOPHY OF WAR AND PEACE. ON THE THRESHOLD OF REVOLUTIONARY CHANGES.

1.1. Towards a qualitatively new philosophical concept of war and peace in contemporary conditions.

The interest in the military phenomena of the modern era is already almost immense. Now not only philosophy and philosophers are looking for an answer to the supreme question of the human race, "to be or not to be", which is aimed at the conceptual worldviews and methodological aspects of this unique problem. Today, the efforts of the world's intellectual potential are concentrated, writers and scientists, doctors and church representatives, even generals from the reserve are looking for a path of reason to life, and at the same time in real life, phenomena are developing in a diametrically opposite way. The preparation of new ones, including star wars, continues at "full steam", as they say, a military flame is constantly streaming in different parts of the planet, the readiness for waging a global missile-nuclear war is complete.

Probably the last one, which if it breaks out will be fought by the last human generation. The planet has truly become like a giant military camp, as if it is about to fight not the war of the century, but something like **the last one. war in its history** . This is approximately how things would look to some intelligent beings from other worlds if they were following the events on our planet.

And at the same time, but not yet adequately, the resistance forces and possibilities of life are growing. History is truly experiencing severe birth pangs, in a world in which everyone must understand that it is necessary for the imperative of survival to be resolutely separated from all kinds of contradictions - class, national, regional, economic, political, ecological, informational and others. Survival is a supreme issue of united humanity, and it cannot be put in danger for the sake of any interests of a more private nature, including class ones.

- **better dead than red** - is absurd , but also its possible reverse modifications, of **the ultra-revolutionary dogmatism** , which has not yet said such a thing, but it is not excluded that individual representatives of it will give verbal preference to a similar, only red, thesis.

To be ready to die for the revolutionary cause, if of course it is necessary, is a highly noble deed, and one that is quite often found in just wars, but to transfer this readiness to all of humanity means that the cause has lost its moral charm and has become the greatest possible absurdity. It is necessary to pay attention to this aspect, not only because in a nuclear war the ratio between the class, the national and the universal changes qualitatively, but also because in the very recent past there was a sad case when in the name of

" **the revolutionary future"** , the lives of 300-350 million human beings were at stake, and from the composition of only one nation, not to mention the small nations, which in such a historical situation should be ready for collective self-sacrifice.

What about all of humanity? No no and no!

In nuclear war, all the opposites of the historical process, justice and injustice, good and evil, sacrifice and self-sacrifice, classes and nations, believers and unbelievers, poor and rich, and so on, merge into a single whole, and it is called non-existence. The deepest philosophical principle in the new political thinking is the idea that these opposites should gather in a world front against death, before universal destruction has gathered them. It is this circumstance that defines the new thinking as **a Philosophy of Life and a Manifesto** to all people and nations, to take part in the struggle to save human civilization. And to the extent that the looming danger is called war, to that extent the worldview and methodological functions of the Marxist-Leninist doctrine have grown immensely, war and the army for peace, and immediately, here we must note that it is precisely this doctrine that has faced the most acute objective need for renewal of its theoretical positions, in accordance with the challenge of the century.

1.2. WAR AS THE OPPOSITE OF THE BASIC PARAMETERS OF HUMAN EXISTENCE. WAR, HUMANISM, REASON.

It is customary to study phenomena in the closest connection with the needs of people. Perhaps not in all cases. Man is the measure of all things, but the assessment of things, that is, the truthful and objective disclosure of their role in human life, is a necessary and natural aspect of knowledge. It remains only to emphasize how strong the desire of people to evaluate war, to reveal its relationship to the basic parameters of existence has been over the millennia. But almost all wars have been synthesized in the laconic formula "a scourge for the nations". Even when victory crowned the end of a war, the victors were forced to heal incurable wounds and overcome the severe consequences of the past storm of military battles. The main characteristic of War, unlike all other social phenomena, is its deep antihuman nature. It is the antithesis of all the basic parameters of human existence and no means of reason are able to dispute this.

War is a destructive force.

It is generally accepted that labor is the source of all wealth. War is a demonic force that either subjects man-made things to open plunder or destroys them. It is it that turns peaceful fields into battlefields. This is its monopoly alone. Countless cities and towns have been subjected to fire and sword, from ancient Troy and Carthage to the enormous destruction of the world wars of the 20th century. Trillions are the measure of the value of those material values that man pays as a terrible tax to this phenomenon.

War is anti-moral.

When it begins, the best thing is to destroy the enemy. The highest forms of "responsibility and duty" are equated with the same. It is a matter of "honor and dignity" to cause the enemy more losses and more suffering. And all this is treated as some special higher form of moral relations.

Even such a great thinker as Hegel undoubtedly was, compares peace to a swamp in which the moral virtues of nations perish, war to a breeze that restores the moral health of people. Thus, even from the point of view of philosophy, it has not been noticed that in a general human plan war means the savagery of morals, and it cannot be viewed in any other way than as anti-moral.

With particular passion and human pain, the antihuman nature of the military element was revealed by Vladimir Ilyich Lenin, through the words: "a brutal massacre in which the bayonet and the bullet , the rope and the fire have their say, a time of endless horrors and suffering, a tragedy of entire nations and world corruption, a wildness after the masses, who choke on blood, when everything is subjected to fire and sword, and people cut each other's throats." (see: Vladimir Ilyich Lenin. Works. Volume 24. Page 430.; Volume 23. Page 11.; Volume 21. Pages 297- 371.)

These are just a small part of the words with which the Great Humanist and Genius Thinker characterizes the moral picture of the First World War carnage.

Perhaps the characterization of war as an anti-moral phenomenon in the life and history of nations will cause certain objections related to the so-called class nature of morality. And as a preventive response, we will note the following: for Marxist-Leninist revolutionary theory, an energetic struggle against abstract morality is characteristic. What is good and fair for some is evil and unfair for others, and the basis of this polarization is class division. All this belongs, as they say, to the alphabetical truths of Marxism-Leninism. However, these considerations do not at all eliminate the big question of universal human values in morality. And especially during wars, when the highest value, namely human life, becomes a hostage to evil. And especially in nuclear war, the existence of all humanity is hostage to it.

In our opinion, Marxist-Leninist ethics still too timidly takes up the question of the qualitatively new relationship between justice and injustice, good and evil in nuclear war. It is still difficult to understand the colossal, what is more, the absolute priority of the universal human and moral principle in this type of war. And it is unlikely that the classics of Marxism-Leninism would allow themselves to ignore the basic fact of this war, that it will act as an absolutely evil force, regardless of who pursues what class goals in it.

War is anti-culture .

(see: Yevtushenko, E. War, this is anticulture. Moscow. 1983)

Discussions can be held about the essence of culture. But it is hardly possible to find any indicator for the inclusion of war in the culture of nations. Nevertheless, there is hardly any other topic that can compete with war in the trace left in the historical tradition of the material and spiritual culture of mankind. Probably every nation has its own "song about the Nibelungs", or poems about Mount Shipka. Not to mention the monuments with which planet Earth is dotted!

War is anti-reason.

And here it can be argued and proven that what is reasonable today may lose this characteristic tomorrow; of course, this is true. But even more important is that, entering into a bloody conflict with the basic parameters of human existence, war ranks among the most unreasonable things in history.

Reason is not just an empty abstraction. It is in labor, in consciousness and in happiness, in knowledge and in joy, in the life and health of people, in the triumph of truth and goodness, in justice and beauty, in all those things that are gathered in the categorical imperative of humanity, where, "Man is a higher being for man."

War is a brutal form of alienation.

Now it is fashionable again to have conversations on the topic of alienation, and to look for the roots and causes of some of its manifestations in relations between people under socialism. Not to mention the disastrous state of alienation in the modern world. The issue, of course, is very important and in no case should we underestimate the deficit in trust and communication that appeared under socialism between young and old, superiors and subordinates, parents and children, towards the state and the party in some socialist countries, between nationalities in one country, minorities and the Majority in a country, and many others that could be listed.

But what can we say about this activity, which Karl Marx called the Human Murder Industry, and in which the humane principle has been banished because it has become dangerous for the successful conduct of war. In war, the object of special attention is the highest human value - his life. For this life, all kinds of weapons have been developed, from arrows to those whose potential power is now measured in new units called "Mega Death", which is equal to 1 million killed human beings. A reasonable humanity that has created a unit of measurement for death that is in Mega?! And this is reason?

The deep and eternal conflict of war with the basic parameters of human existence is one of the main reasons why human knowledge has been powerless for centuries to discover the truth about its essence and role in history. Despite the almost continuous millennial movement of this Bloody Carousel, as some Soviet authors call it, human knowledge could not go further than mysticism and irrationalism in its explanation. And until the middle of the nineteenth century, war remained something of a black box, and even worse. Various representatives of human thought have tried to penetrate its secrets - philosophers and political figures, prominent military leaders and scientists, writers, poets, church figures. The philosophical views created about its essence and the programs for its elimination from the lives of peoples are endless. But until the emergence of Marxist-Leninist doctrine, the true essence of wars remained hidden from social knowledge. All possible programs for its elimination from the life of nations also proved to be useless. At best, these were utopian sighs for peace, which were called pacifism.

Naturally, the question arises, what is the reason for, what explains this prolonged theoretical and practical helplessness of humanity in the face of warriors?

We have already addressed one of the main reasons, the epistemological one, related to the almost antinomic nature of its contradictions with the basic definitions of human existence. However, there is another reason of a more general nature.

In the broadest theoretical sense, this is also explained by the lack of objective conditions. Thus, both Marxism-Leninism as a revolutionary theory of the working class and the scientific Theory of War and its practical overcoming were waiting for their historical time.

More specifically, the dominant exploiting classes have created insurmountable objective and subjective difficulties. The interests of these classes usually coincide with the conduct of all kinds of predatory wars. In them and through them, they have satisfied a part of their insatiable thirst for wealth. History knows no more striking case in this respect than the modern military-industrial complex. For thousands of years, this thinking either took war under more open protection, or did the same, but in deeply disguised forms. As for the real opponents of war, expressing, albeit in a utopian form, the interests and anti-war sentiments of the masses of the people, they have usually been subjected to cruel persecution. Under capitalism, this state of affairs has been preserved to this day.

1.3. IS THE MARXIST-LENINIST APPROACH TO MILITARY PHENOMENA IN HISTORY OUTDATED?

At the modern stage, certain opportunities have arisen to question and declare the class-party approach to military phenomena obsolete and outmoded; moreover, in its most radical form, this opportunity can grow into a denial of the class approach to contemporary social processes in general. There are already quite a few bourgeois ideologists and political figures who view the restructuring of socialism and the new political thinking as evidence that socialism has collapsed, that social practice has not confirmed the basic idea of Marxism-Leninism, to create a classless society, as the revolutionary vocal energy of the working class is being used. But the problem is not only with the position of bourgeois ideologists, which position is in many respects deliberate and can be viewed as a modern variant of an older, and generally familiar, ideological attitude towards Marxism-Leninism.

The question of the class nature of the perestroika and the new political thinking is now gaining significant importance. How to understand the class approach, since life itself, the new historical realities of recent decades have brought to the fore more acute general human problems and, above all, the absolute question of the survival of humanity. Is the class approach correct in this unusual historical situation? Isn't it more logical to refer it to those approaches that undermine the unity, mutual dependence, and common destiny of the modern world? Isn't it more correct, in the interests of this common destiny, to take on the character of a special imperative, to abandon this approach as incompatible with the new historical content of the world in which we live. Especially when it comes to military phenomena, in which there is a completely unusual danger of self-destruction of the human race. The logic of these questions goes even further. Because in theoretical terms, it is about the main thing in Marxism, what Vladimir Ilyich Lenin called the greatest conquest of universal scientific thought. It is about the historical mission of the working class and the proletarian class-party approach as an ideological, political, military means for the historical realization of this mission. Has all this become obsolete in the conditions of new historical realities? In essence, it is a question of the fate of Marxism today, which is also faced with the notorious dilemma of Hamlet: "to be or not to be."

Perhaps the form of this question is not yet so radical and almost challenging, but the need for a revolutionary renewal of this theory is more than undeniable.

As for the analysis of military phenomena, the question of the class approach to them and the limitations that have arisen for its application in contemporary conditions cannot be resolved only within the scope of one question, even if it is the most important, fundamental, and most important one, such as the question of the military aspects of the survival of humanity.

The thing is that this issue is very much like the surface part of an iceberg, on which the underwater part is hidden and the extreme complexity of war, this "extremely colorful phenomenon", as Vladimir Ilyich Lenin called it.

To avoid atomic destruction is an absolutely necessary imperative of the time. But the realization of this only reasonable perspective can hardly be realized without an accurate, scientific and class analysis of the processes from which the Monster of atomic "homocide" was born. These are processes in which many forces contributed to humanity ending up where it should never have been. But what can be said, since every contribution to this satanic process had a deep class character and that this state of affairs continues to be objectively preserved. Because desires are one thing, and objective processes are another. And even more imperative now, in the conditions of new historical realities, is to take into account the warning of Vladimir Ilyich Lenin that there is no more dangerous mistake than mixing desires with the objective characteristics of things. Including when it comes to such a, let's call it "poisonous", issue for modern humanity, as the issue of war. For its universal human and class aspects. About the objective need for universal and class, national and supranational, regional, and other possible approaches to it, about the historical and contemporary dialectics of these approaches, about their subordination and coordination, in contemporary political and military political practice.

In a broader philosophical and methodological plan, it is impossible to ignore the historical role of the class approach to wars, first applied by Karl Marx and Friedrich Engels. This is impossible not only from the point of view of historical truth. Rather, it is necessary for modern military-political practice, as a theoretical reference point that will retain its role until the last soldier on this planet takes off his uniform.

As is known, until the middle of the 19th century, the military history of mankind was most often "illuminated" and sanctified by religion. The scientific approach to military phenomena, as well as the prerequisites for its application, were lacking. Objective historical conditions for creating a scientific theory of wars arose with the emergence of the working class, and more specifically with the transformation of the working class into an independent force of history. These conditions are concluded, first of all, in the fact that, by its objective characteristics and interests, the working class is alien to wars. In its historical mission of building a classless society, the abolition of wars is inextricably linked and follows by force of law from the abolition of exploitation and oppression.

On the basis of these objective conditions, a real possibility for a scientific approach to wars appeared. It was realized in the general system of Marxism - Leninism and with particular force in historical materialism. And now, when the trends of modern historical development are giving priority to universal human values, it is hardly right to forget that "Marx's historical materialism," as Vladimir Ilyich Lenin emphasized, "is the greatest achievement of scientific thought. The chaos and arbitrariness that had reigned until then in views on history and views on politics have been replaced by a strikingly complete and harmonious scientific theory." (See: Vladimir Ilyich Lenin. Collected Works. Second Edition. Volume 23. Page 44.)

This coherent, comprehensive and strikingly scientific theory already contained within itself a methodological possibility for overcoming the chaos and arbitrariness in the views on war. Of course, in this respect too, Marxism inherited and raised to a new historical level the humanistic traditions of the struggle against war, which, although in the form of utopian pacifism, are found throughout human history. As a Philosophy of History, expressing the interests of the working class, historical materialism could not leave out of its field of vision such an acute social problem as war. In this sense, historical materialism also contains within itself the philosophy of war. More precisely, it is the only philosophical theoretical foundation in which social knowledge has found sound methodological principles for the scientific study of military phenomena, for arming **all peoples, all anti-military classes, anti-military social strata, and all forces of peace with an efficient, scientifically-based theory and program** , for combating the modern forces of war, and in the future, for the complete exclusion of wars from the life of peoples.

From the general system of these principles, the first place should be given to the requirement for a class-party approach to military phenomena, which must be in **inseparable unity** with the need:

all humanity to be freed from war .

This principle is a kind of methodological core of historical materialism and on this basis can be defined as the supreme principle, thanks to which war has ceased to be a mystery for human knowledge. It played the role of a kind of key to penetrate the most complex and difficult problems of war, relating to the causes of its occurrence, to its essence and to the factors on which its character depends, as well as the historical destiny that Vladimir Ilyich Lenin points out, of the Marxist doctrine of the historical role of the working class. He defines this doctrine as the most important moment in the general system of Marxism, from which also follows the requirement that all social phenomena be considered from the positions of the proletarian point of view.

"The main thing in Marx's teachings," Vladimir Ilyich Lenin emphasized, "is the clarification of the world historical role of the proletariat as the builder of socialist society."

Transferred and applied to war, this situation means that **the path to eternal peace between peoples** passes along the same revolutionary paths along which the working class fulfills its historical mission. Thus, peace from a centuries-old, mysterious and unattainable antipode of war turned into a scientifically based strategic slogan in the struggle for a classless society. And all this was called **the proletarian class-party approach or the proletarian point of view.**

The historical mission of the working class in this regard is shown with a certain clarity in the thought of Karl Marx that

" In place of the old society with its economic poverty and political madness, the proletariat will build a new society in which human labor will be the sole ruler, and eternal peace will prevail in relations between nations."

But in order for this to happen, it is necessary to "overthrow all the relations in which Man is a humiliated, enslaved, helpless being." (see: Karl Marx. Friedrich Engels. Works. Volume One. Page 407.). In the context of war, we can also add a killed being. The class approach has become a powerful methodological tool of social science. Among many other things, thanks to it, the internal connection between the emergence of war and the emergence of classes was discovered, and therefore the destruction of classes as a necessary objective prerequisite for the elimination of wars from the life of peoples. This very position is the guiding methodological thread, under the sign of which socialism solved and solves both the problems of its military defense and the complex issues of the fight against the military danger in general.

The class-party approach does not contradict the need for a specific historical study of each individual war. On the contrary, it contains within itself the requirement to reveal the specific **class causes of wars** , the specific class connection by virtue of which a given policy turns into war, and the specific voicing factors that determine its character. Without a specific approach, these general questions of each war cannot be correctly resolved. But even the most specific approach is doomed to unprincipled wanderings if it does not take into account the struggle between classes, that is, if it considers the war outside and independently of this struggle. Even microscopic deviations in this respect can prove fatal for the forces that have made such a mistake.

Here is a Leninist statement that revealed its methodological charge with new force in contemporary conditions:

"Whoever tackles private issues without first resolving general ones will inevitably, at every step, unconsciously encounter these general issues. And to confront someone with them in every particular case means dooming his policy to the worst wanderings and unprincipledness."

However, it is necessary to bring complete clarity to the dialectic of the general and the particular in the wars of the modern era, and especially the missile-nuclear one. Because the relative weight of its specific problems has grown to such an extent that reasonable doubts have arisen as to whether this is a war at all?

This is the meaning of Mikhail Gorbachev's words when he wrote:

"This isn't even really a war... This is suicide."

(see: Mikhail Gorbachev. Perestroika and new thinking for us and for the whole world. 1987. Page 175.)

In this situation, the class-party approach to the war was facing serious tests. There was a real danger of a dogmatic application of this approach to the new historical realities, as well as of a reserved attitude towards it, which has already been discussed.

The universal human problems of missile and nuclear war proved to be particularly difficult for class analysis. They are inherent in every war, but nuclear war brought them to the forefront, and posed with great sharpness the question of the priority of universal human values and, above all, the incomparable question of **the survival of humanity** .

In this peculiar critical situation, the Marxist-Leninist, class-party approach to the contemporary state and prospects of military phenomena fully retains its strength, but at the same time it is becoming increasingly clear that **it can no longer be applied as before, that objective conditions have matured for qualitative changes in its content** . Otherwise, this approach, despite its proven scientific advantages, will turn into unnecessary dogmatism, manifestations of which, by the way, are already occurring.

The class-party approach is an indispensable methodological weapon of historical materialism in the fight against unscientific philosophical, socialist and other doctrines of war.

War is not only an extremely complex issue. It is at the same time a phenomenon enjoying a special **ideological protection from the classes interested in it** . It is clear that wars are always and only waged by the masses. But in order to be involved in it, they must receive a certain minimum of ideological opium, that is, to obtain in their thinking the illusion that no one but they are interested in the war. This is the main reason that has brought social knowledge of wars to a disastrous state. Military history has found itself under the power of the same **ideological and metaphysical chaos** that has dominated all of human history.

From its very inception, historical materialism entered into a courageous and uncompromising struggle with the class ideological distortions of military phenomena. In contemporary conditions, this methodological role of historical materialism has grown even more, insofar as **the prevention of war, before its first shots are fired, will depend to a decisive extent on the ideological position of the peoples, on the extent to which they will develop within themselves forces of resistance** against the contemporary ideological avalanche of militarism, hegemonism and other numerous new and old "isms" with which the forces of war hide their ugly and terrible face. (See: Volkogonov. Psychological War. Sofia. 1986. Pages 227, 270.)

1.4. SOCIO-ECONOMIC FORMATION. WAR AND HISTORY. THE IMPERATIVE OF PEACE IN THE MODERN WORLD.

One of the great questions of the knowledge of war is the question of its connections and dependencies with the economy, politics, science and technology, with various forms of public consciousness, with ideology and the human psyche. This is a complex question, the correct answer to which allows one to see the place of war in the general system of the socio-economic formation and of history. Bourgeois philosophical and sociological thought has created, and continues to create, an abundance of points of view, the incurable disease of which is the class arbitrariness in considering the relationship between war and other social phenomena. Some bring to the fore the relationship war-technology, others emphasize the relationship politics-war, and still others give preference to ideological factors.

Almost constantly reproduced a large group of theories in which the emphasis is placed on the natural origin of war, and its social essence is denied. It is necessary to emphasize (This is especially important!) that this chaos of mutually differing, and sometimes, fighting points of view, does not speak of the intellectual poverty of bourgeois ideologists. Rather, it is evidence of class inferiority, which shows that the objective truth on these issues is the only thing the bourgeoisie fears, and this is precisely what condemns it to a lifelong alliance with lies. In modern conditions it has become the "shadow of Horace" of bourgeois thinking, draped in the mantle of anti-Sovietism.

Historical materialism is a qualitatively new revolutionary philosophical and methodological basis for studying war in the general system of socio-economic formations, for revealing its objective and independent of the will and desires of people, its connections with economics, politics, culture and spiritual phenomena, for the mutual subordination of these connections and dependencies.

As is known, the Marxist-Leninist Philosophy of History is a materialist and dialectical philosophy. Strictly adhering to the basic idea of materialism about the primacy of Matter over consciousness, Karl Marx and Friedrich Engels came to the conclusion about the Independence and the determining role of social existence over social consciousness. Further, social existence was identified with the social material conditions of people's life, and the mode of production turned out to be their core and at the same time the basis of the entire human history. This new approach did not allow material phenomena and relations in history to be explained by political or spiritual reasons. On the contrary, the methodologically new approach obliged political and Spiritual phenomena, processes and relations to be explained by the state and changes in social existence and, above all, by the mode of production. With this, a Copernican revolution was carried out in social science.

It became clear what the real basis of history is, what and why it is set on it, by what laws the mode of production changes, how those new sides, contradictions and tendencies arise within it, from which subsequently, with the force of law, corresponding changes occur in the superstructural political, legal, spiritual and other strata of society.

In short, it was an approach in which every social phenomenon found its own place and historical development became a natural-historical process. These fundamental ideas of historical materialism became a qualitatively new logic and method for studying military phenomena. In the spirit of their methodological research, the determining role of the mode of production and its relation to war was revealed in the foreground and above all. In its sphere, in its inherent contradictions, that necessity with which the origin of wars is genetically connected and which for a certain period of human history makes them inevitable is brought. But in this same sphere there is also the possibility of abolishing wars. In a certain state of the productive forces and production relations, this possibility becomes a reality and humanity forever parted with wars. This approach dealt an irresistible blow to the mystically veiled view of the eternity of wars, while at the same time significantly strengthening the optimism and faith of the peoples that a world without wars is possible. Of significant methodological importance is the historical materialist requirement to take into account two types of connections between the mode of production and war. On the one hand, the influence they exert on it by the vital forces, and on the other, the influence of the relations of production. In both cases, one can speak of direct and indirect influence, due to the two-sided nature of this interaction.

The main thing, however, is the differentiated approach to the influence of the productive forces and production relations on military phenomena, which is this methodological thread that provided new opportunities for social knowledge and military science for a deeper, more versatile and more accurate coverage of the causes and laws of the development of military affairs. From a historical materialist point of view, the productive forces are a kind of umbilical cord of the means of warfare, and the latter determine the forms and methods of armed struggle. The main thing in it is the law of the correspondence of the ways, forms and methods of existing, and ceaselessly changing means. This law confronts socialist military science with the need to most carefully monitor the revolutionary changes in modern productive forces and the influence they have on the means of armed struggle and, on this basis, to promptly introduce the necessary changes in the forms and methods of conducting battle, the operation and the war as a whole. In the conditions of the scientific and technological revolution, violating this requirement can lead to significantly more serious consequences than under other conditions. Here, we will open, as they say, a small parenthesis to ask an extremely important question:

What does missile and nuclear war look like through the prism of the productive forces from which modern means of armed struggle were born?

Isn't this a typical example of a dialectical negation of the phenomenon of war, a negation that is carried out in the deepest depths of social existence?

Some authors rightly raise the question of **the complete uselessness of the atomic bomb, since it cannot achieve any reasonable combat goals, and moreover, with the massive use of nuclear weapons, the protection of one's troops and peoples from the devastating properties of one's own nuclear explosions becomes absurd** .

This question has acquired fundamental importance, not only for military science, but also for the dialectics of war with politics in the modern era. However, it is not logical to conclude from this absurdity that the problems of the military defense of socialism have also become meaningless. This is an illusory connection with which some authors conceal their unwillingness to accept the profound qualitative changes that have occurred in the relationship between war and politics. The military defense of socialism is a perfectly real and not an absurd question, but its modern historical content has undergone such great changes under the influence of armaments and military equipment that the following can definitely be stated: **if it becomes necessary, as in past wars, for socialism to defend its interests with the power of nuclear weapons, then precisely in such a case, its military defense will no longer be possible and absurd.** Such a view may seem unacceptable to some, but the absolute power of nuclear missiles does not give us any reason to retain in **the content of the concept of military defense** its most important component so far:

The idea of conducting successful military operations, until complete victory over the enemy. Now in this concept, in our opinion, the strategic task of not reaching the combat use of nuclear missile weapons, which has two aspects, acquires priority importance:

First, both sides should stop striving for military superiority and unilaterally guaranteeing military security.

Secondly , even more reliable than the first, to proceed with the complete destruction of this weapon, as a technical imperative of the modern concept of military security.

The nature of the dependences between war and production relations is different. Of course, they also have a certain influence on the forms and methods of armed struggle. The main thing, however, is that production relations contain in themselves that methodological connection which alone is able to explain the origin and historical limits of wars. Production relations are relations of interests, more precisely the most concentrated form of economic interests which, under conditions of private ownership of the means of production, tirelessly and objectively divide people into large groups called classes, as one of them, the minority exploits the others. On the basis of this relationship of exploitation of man by man, political and legal forms of violence, alienation and hatred and all sorts of other social diseases arise. Private property is the roots of wars , and its emergence and elimination outlines the historical limits of this social disaster. But with one reservation of a modern nature, that the elimination of the danger of nuclear war must occur long before the destruction of capitalism. Private property is not some fiction or an economic deity standing above people.

It is in the hands of certain people and in fact all the evils that come from it are evils of these hands. All this explains why the reason that controls these hands, that is, the consciousness of the exploiting classes, makes enormous efforts to veil the relationship between private property and war, and to remove responsibility from the forces of militarism.

The historical materialist theory of the essence and historical types of production relations is the methodological basis of the scientific approach to the causes, essence and character of wars, which is applied in the Marxist-Leninist doctrine of war and the army. A significant methodological role is played by historical materialism in the theoretical analysis of the war-politics relationship. In modern conditions, this relationship has proven to be tense, as they say "to the extreme limit". On the one hand, there is the enormous responsibility of politics for the future of humanity refracted through the prism of the Nuclear Imperative. On the other hand, in the theoretical tradition of the Marxist-Leninist concept of war, the relation **"War is a continuation of politics" is presented very strongly and in an inseparable form** . On the other hand, speculations on this issue by bourgeois ideologists, revisionists and others do not cease. There are sufficient grounds for dogmatism to become more active, which, by the way, is already being observed, including at the philosophical level. All this requires separating the decisions of the past from what corresponds to the new realities. Obviously, even in modern conditions, the theoretical analysis of this issue must be consistent with the essence of politics, which, on the one hand, is a concentrated expression of the economy, but on the other, holds in its hands the main part of the management functions, which provides it with a very large, and recently, increasing, relative independence in relation to the entire socio-economic formation, including the economic base on which it is based.

The revolutionary role of historical materialism is also immutable for the objective scientific analysis of the place and role of spiritual phenomena and factors of a given society in war. And in this area, idealism and metaphysics have left behind traces of class-calculated, subjective arbitrariness. What has not been attributed to Spiritual phenomena - from the causes of wars to the magical ability of reason (religious, philosophical, moral) to eliminate wars. For historical materialism, Spiritual phenomena, that is, social and individual consciousness, are a reflection of a subjective image of social material conditions, more precisely, of social existence. In the spiritual sphere, ideological, psychic, conscious or subconscious, there are no and cannot be reasons for wars. But in every war, spiritual factors also operate. This is a law of human activity , and this law operates not according to the choice of the combatants, but according to the goals they have set for themselves, and when these goals are humane, humane and just, then Spiritual factors manifest enormous power and become a kind of "terrible kind of weapon."

The historical materialist doctrine of the essence and role of Spiritual factors in history is the methodological basis of education in the socialist armies. It is called upon to forge in the personnel a fighting spirit of a new historical type, models of which were shown in the wars of the Soviet peoples against imperialism. One can only regret that individual commanders, either due to insufficient methodological preparation and culture or due to weaknesses of a voluntaristic nature, do not pay due attention to precisely those advantages that history itself has placed on the side of the socialist armies. The most frequent evidence of this is the perversions of disciplinary practice. Ultimately, referred to the history of society, war is a natural phenomenon for those social systems in the economic basis of which lies the exploitation of man by man. The deepest root of wars is the economic fall of private property, which throughout the history of antagonistic societies has gone hand in hand with the political fall, violence, including its most brutal form in the face of wars. And of course, to this union of economics and politics with war, the thinking of the exploiters and oppressors is also added. Reason has never been able to provide effective protection for peoples from the horrors of war. All this is true, and has been confirmed thousands of times in real wars. But when it comes to the modern era, in addition to the unconditional connection of war with economic, political, ideological, moral and scientific and technical factors, the role of two more factors must be taken into account: first, socialism and second, the striking capabilities of modern weapons.

Both factors reveal a real prospect of eliminating War from the life of nations even before the demise of capitalism and the development of socialism throughout the world. As a matter of knowledge, this prospect is very complex and contradictory, and as a goal of political strategy, its realization will for a long time encounter the resistance of imperialism and the danger of war, which radiates the aggressive nature of capitalism. But there is sufficient reason to assume that, faced with the threat of universal destruction, humanity will find the right path to a world without weapons, to security and reliable peace, for all peoples regardless of the differences in their social and state systems. And in this question the powerful influence of the new historical content of the world is felt.

In the past, it was believed that the main feature of relations between two historically neighboring socio-economic formations is the endless confrontation that continues until the complete and final victory of one of them. Approximately according to the same scenario, relations between capitalism and socialism developed, the main formula of these relations was the notorious question : **"who to whom?"** and all this had some justification for its time. And history could hardly have avoided these exceptional in their strength class clashes from the initial period of the emergence of socialism.

Now, however, the times and above all the material foundations and conditions of the relations between capitalism and socialism are radically different from that initial period. Socialism is already a system that cannot be defeated by war and, as a system, has won its historical right to exist alongside capitalism. **On the other hand, socialism must also distinguish itself from the dogmatic prejudice that the demise of capitalism is almost imminent . Particularly dangerous is the military modification of this** prejudice, which had penetrated even into program documents as a prediction that **capitalism would perish** in a third world war, including a nuclear one, and naturally from the blows of the military power of socialism.

The philosophical and methodological point of view allows us to admit and subject to dialectical analysis the idea that socialism as a socio-economic system has lost the battle with capitalism and has disappeared from the face of the planet Earth. Does this mean that the threat of a nuclear apocalypse will automatically disappear and the nuclear arsenal will be buried for "eternal times", since the threat of the "mortal enemy" called socialism no longer exists?! No! This is a deadly dangerous utopia, because in the "soul" of capitalism "a demonic force rages", for supremacy, for power, for large and super-large profits, for the conquest of neighboring peoples, for the appropriation of new territories, for the exploitation of new natural wealth and resources, for the satisfaction of all imperial ambitions, which is imperialism in its complete form, which leads to militarism in its complete form, which leads to the creation of ever more perfect, more efficient conventional and nuclear weapons, with the sole purpose of taking human life. New historical realities direct the modern historical process, from the formula "who whom" to the diametrically opposite principle, to learn the great art of "living together", which means that peace between peoples and social systems is also becoming one of the imperatives of the time, and in all likelihood for a very long historical period.

1.5. MAIN FEATURES OF THE MARXIST-LENINIST DOCTRINE OF WAR PEACE AND THE ARMY IN ITS CLASSICAL FORM.

On the theoretical basis of historical materialism, Marxist-Leninist philosophy developed its own conceptual view of wars in history. We will abstract from the old question of what relation the three components of Marxism have to the emergence and historical development of this view and will take only the philosophical aspect, that is, only those of its features which in their totality are something like the Philosophy of War and Peace. The scale of this doctrine, or more precisely its internal necessary structure, is determined by the own limits of historical materialism as the Philosophy of History. And since war, as a rule, is a more or less complete state of society, the Marxist-Leninist doctrine of war and the army in its classical form contains within itself a very wide range of problems affecting all sides of a given socio-economic formation. Here is a part of these problems: the economic basis of wars;; War and nature;;; War and the masses of the people; war and revolution progressed, with War and generals, War and science, War and politics, War and classes, war, state and nation, War and religion, War and law, War and morality, War and way of life, of people and so on. These are not artificial questions and every war in human history has created tension, not only in individual links in the entire chain of the mentioned questions, that is, in the overall state of society.

The synthetic methodological characteristic of the Marxist-Leninist doctrine of war and peace will allow us to avoid any difficulties in the transition to the qualitatively new Philosophy of War and Peace, which is contained in the new political thinking and which can be fully deservedly considered as a historically new stage in the development of the Marxist-Leninist philosophical concept of war. So what are the main most characteristic features of the Marxist-Leninist doctrine of war Peace and the army, and how are they interconnected in a systematized overall view?

First:

War is an extremely diverse and extremely complex social phenomenon.

This feature, which Vladimir Ilyich Lenin dwells on in his lecture on war, read during the First World War, has at least three meanings: first, the great depth and sharpness of the contradictions that it resolves and the unusual means that are used for this purpose. Second, in the sense of human activity, which really cannot be compared with anything, neither in tension and means, nor in the ideological and psychological appearance of the warring people, nor in the final results, and third, the archetype is motley in the ways of interaction with all systems and subsystems of society, economy, science, technology, politics, ideology, culture, and others. It is precisely the war that is this factor that weaves into one knot all sides of the life of the warring states, weaves very much in such a way that the years of the war and some time after are years of deep crisis and difficult-to-heal wounds. These are years in which many classes, political movements and personalities, and sometimes entire social systems, suffer heavy defeats. It is in this connection that Friedrich Engels predicted that in a World Carnage a dozen crowns would fall into the dust, and there would be no one to pick them up. By the way, history after that, and even before that, has more than once confirmed the words of the great thinker. It is enough to recall how the Second World War ended for the leaders of fascism in Germany. Taken together, these three meanings of the complexity of war occupy a certain place in its objective specificity and have a significant impact on the development of the subjective attitude towards it and, above all, the military-political and military-ideological strategy. And here we will immediately provoke philosophical, and not only philosophical, thought with the following question: what subjective strategy is necessary if the complexity of war has acquired dimensions bordering on the absurd, and if it has turned into an equation of non-existence? This question cannot be ignored. It is criminal to subject oneself to deliberate and ideological speculation, as reactionary circles in the West do, but it is not allowed to submit to outdated positions, as, by the way, some dogmatically inclined representatives of Marxist-Leninist, military philosophical thought still do.

Second , *each war must be examined specifically* .

"To be a Marxist - emphasizes Vladimir Ilyich Lenin, you must assess each war concretely." (Vladimir Ilyich Lenin Works Volume 23 page 27). In fact, concreteness is the general form of manifestation of complexity or, more precisely, the historical scale on which the complexity of each war is plotted. For example, the Punic Wars are something very different from the wars of the Bulgarians against Byzantium, not to mention the peculiarities of machine wars. And it is precisely concreteness that is this sign in response to which Vladimir Ilyich Lenin raises a precisely defined principle: "One should not approach with a general template" (Vladimir Ilyich Lenin Works Volume 23 page 27). And at the same time, however, in the infinite diversity of wars Lenin draws attention to "two main and root streams" as he expresses it, namely "the objective content of the war" and "the subjective ideology of the class" that leads it.

They are precisely that common thing which is concretized in a unique way in each individual war. From the dialectical unity of these two streams, the subjective and the objective, a third characteristic feature of the Marxist-Leninist concept of war is formed, finding expression in an extremely important fundamental question!

Third:

Who prepared a given war and why?

Without this question, no war can be understood , which means that an adequate political attitude towards it is impossible.

Moreover, this question, "why a given war broke out, which classes waged it, what historical and historical-economic conditions caused it," Lenin characterized as the "fundamental question" of the doctrine of war.

Here is his statement in verbatim form:

"From the point of view of Marxism, the main problem in discussing the question of how the war should be evaluated and what our attitude towards it should be lies in what this war is being fought for, which classes have prepared it." (Lenin Vladimir Ilyich Volume 24, Page 405).

Fourth:

War is not a historical phenomenon .

The fundamental question of war unties one of the Gordian knots of war, in which its connection with history was hidden. Through the prism of this question, several fundamental questions were scientifically illuminated: first, that war is not a supra-historical phenomenon. It arises at a certain stage of human history, in close connection with specific historical and economic conditions, in which the most important place is occupied by the emergence of private property, class division, exploitation and oppression of man by man.

It is the most uglier form of violence, which is applied to entire peoples for economic gain .

It is for her that Friedrich Engels' thought is most appropriate:

"Violence is only a means, the goal is economic gain." (Karl Marx, Friedrich Engels. Works. Volume 20. Pages 161-162).

In its own historical process, war, like an "umbilical cord", has been tied to economic benefit, but the specific form of this connection has turned out to be extremely diverse. Caesar's slave campaigns in Europe or the Persian Wars against ancient Greece, the Wars of Alexander the Great or the Crusades, the Wars of the Turkish Empire or the endless wars with the help of which the notorious Empire of colonies was created, the two World Wars, dozens of regional wars After World War II, in general, these nearly 15 thousand wars, fought over several thousand years, have only been connected to economic benefit in different ways. And just as the laws of nature are not written in the sky, in the same way, no war has written on its flag the economic benefit it pursues. The deep and natural connection of war with economic benefit undergoes qualitative changes under socialism. On the economic basis of public property, he breaks the millennial connection of exploitative economic benefit with the waging of wars. Under socialism, no social group can receive any benefit whatsoever from war against other peoples. If there is such an aspiration, this is no longer socialism. The most eloquent example of such a deception was National Socialism in Germany, which, under the auspices of "socialism", tried to realize completely absurd forms of World Economic and Political Domination of the German Monopolies. However, it is naive to believe that the attitude of socialism to war is built outside and independently of economic benefit. For example, on a moral or some other basis. Among other things, such a thesis would suffer from an idealistic explanation of the connection between socialism and war. The thing is that for socialism it is economically profitable not to have wars at all, and this benefit is qualitatively different from the economic interest in wars inherent in private property. This is a historically new type of economic benefit, which is realized in the "subjective stream" of war in the form of a political strategy of peaceful relations between peoples regardless of their social and state system. This is precisely how Vladimir Ilyich Lenin's statement that the ideal of socialism is peace should be understood. But in this ideal, a new historical regularity is essentially expressed: friendship and cooperation between peoples, which in fact puts an end to wars. Special attention needs to be paid to the consideration of the issue of the economic benefit of capitalism and socialism from military clashes between them. Judging by the experience of World War II, American monopolies realized a benefit that has no equal in world history. But on this issue, the leaders and ideologists of modern America do not want to have a conversation.

If we judge by the logic of private property and its most prominent representatives, the billionaires of all nationalities, it is economically advantageous for socialism to not exist in this world at all. Socialism would also prefer a society in which all peoples have made their choice in favor of socialist public property, because it is precisely this perspective that conceals unsuspected opportunities for a unified approach to the economic interests of all peoples. This is, so to speak, the optimal option for economic benefit, from which the causes of wars are forever removed. However, if we judge by the logic of modern historical realities, it is economically most advantageous for socialism and capitalism to establish peaceful relations of mutual economic benefit. Because in the flames of a nuclear war, any benefit will be extinguished, and besides, the preparation for it has already become an unbearable burden for the peoples. Only the military-industrial complex is looking for the so-called new markets and money, in the direction of the military business, but in the end, even its leaders should understand that this direction leads to the Abyss of Non-existence. Obviously, we have every reason to believe that mutually beneficial economic cooperation of countries and peoples with different social state systems is an economic imperative of the time, a factor on which the complete normalization of international relations and the elimination of the Nuclear Nightmare will depend to a decisive extent. Such is, by the way, the deep meaning of the ideology of interstate relations and the separation of the question of the peaceful coexistence of capitalism and socialism from the theory and practice of the class struggle. However, the question of the objective presence of the class moment in the historically established relations and conflicts between the two powerful modern social systems and the way in which this objectivity acquired a corresponding subjective political form during the different periods after the victory of the Great October Socialist Revolution remains open. Because if the new theoretical propositions arising from the new historical realities are accepted with old prescription, an unacceptable discrepancy can result with the colossal class hatred with which the leaders of capitalism greeted the birth of the new social order. This was a class struggle in the true sense of the word, in which socialism also defended its historical right from class positions. As for peaceful coexistence in the sense that Vladimir Ilyich Lenin gave it and which has now come to the fore, it is more logical to assume that it was not established at all due to the lack of objective conditions. Things may change now, but the class subtext of the relations between the two social systems will objectively be preserved, albeit with a dominant role of universal human values. The question is the management of this subtext , to make it subject to political means

Fifth:

War is a continuation of politics, by violent means.

Of all the connections of war with the socio-economic formation, Vladimir Ilyich Lenin pays the most significant attention to the attitude towards politics. He singles it out as the Essence of war, which is subjectively reflected and fixed in the widely known definition that it is a continuation of the policy of certain interested states and the classes within them by violent means. Now, when it is precisely in this definition that the need for a radical turn to a qualitatively new, also deeply revolutionary solution to the fundamental question of the dialectics of war is outlined, it is necessary to observe strict objectivity to the historical truth surrounding this question. It is about what is the attitude of Vladimir Ilyich Lenin, and a little earlier also of Friedrich Engels, to this question and its various aspects. Because if the transition to a new solution to this old and present question is motivated by the fact that Clausewitz's definition is outdated, without even mentioning not the point of view, but the name of

Lenin, the feeling arises that something is wrong with historical truth. That is why it is necessary, albeit in a laconic form, to see what Lenin said, and then to assess to what extent what was said has retained its force in relation to the specifics of nuclear war. Surely the Great Leader of the Revolution will not be "angry" if those who then call themselves Leninists are able not only to study his teachings, but also to develop them creatively, especially at turning points in the development of human history.

"The basic proposition of dialectics," Lenin wrote, "is that war is simply a continuation of politics by other, namely violent means." This was always the point of view of Marx and Engels, who viewed every war as a continuation of the policy of certain interested states, and of the various classes within them, at a given time. And further: "It would be theoretically quite wrong to forget that every war is merely a continuation of politics by other means." (Vladimir Ilyich Lenin, Works, Volume 21, page 211). And let us immediately pose one of the most delicate questions: If someone, whoever he is, now, in modern conditions, in the analysis of nuclear war forgets this proposition of Lenin, will we still be dealing with a theoretically quite erroneous point of view? But we could also pose the question in another way: Is such a war possible in which precisely this point of view becomes erroneous and politically dangerous? It is quite obvious that the delicacy of these questions stems from the way in which the names of Marx, Engels and Lenin are committed to the view that war is a continuation of politics. It seems that this circumstance also has a certain influence on modern disputes about the dialectics of politics, with the preparation and conduct of not just any war, but a missile-nuclear war. We will pay special attention to this issue later. Here we will only note the following: there is only one point of view that the classics of Marxism-Leninism recognized as absolute. This is the point of view of living life. Relative to it, all other points of view are variables , and this applies in full force to the relations of war with politics.

The main features of the Marxist-Leninist philosophical doctrine of war, Peace and the Army, outlined in this way played a huge methodological role in the policy of the Soviet state after the victory of the Great October Socialist Revolution. It was on this theoretical basis that the military-political strategy of the Soviet Union was developed and implemented in practice. Not in the first years, but in the first days and hours of Soviet power, it was clear that imperialism would not ignore the Huge breakthrough in its World System. It became clear that all kinds of efforts, including military ones, would follow to stifle the breakthrough. It became clear that the conductor of these efforts would be politics, and the goal - economic benefit from the vast Russian markets, sources of raw materials, living spaces, and what not. In greater depth, that economic benefit that is associated with the protection of the historical positions of private property on the entire planet. Everything was as if according to a scenario: an unusual victory of a Deep Class Revolution and the usual reaction of its class, internal and external enemies. After the economic Blockades, sanitary and other corridors did not give any result, it was the turn of the weapon. The most suitable force for the purpose was found, German fascism. A plan for the most sinister military conflagration in history, global in its scale, unsurpassed in its victims and destruction, unparalleled in the manifestations of class sadism, flared up as a continuation of politics. And when everything did not end according to the expectations of those who prepared it, the most unprecedented, steepest, most contradictory stage in the development of military history began, a stage of the self-denial of militarism, which, however, was carried out according to the terrible formula of the noble Barbarians of antiquity, who buried their loved ones alive upon their death. And so, Step by Step, humanity reached non-symbolically, is real to the great philosophical and life question: to be or not to be? And it is hardly permissible in this historical situation to rely on the rational formula "Everything will pass by itself". A formula that awakens justified anxiety in many scientists, because it speaks of the lack of an adequate, emotional, moral and political position towards the danger of the Nuclear Apocalypse. And precisely this, as some call it "herd state" of huge masses of people, is seen as a striking phenomenon and an extremely important moment of the Nuclear Problem. Thus, with many problems and difficulties, the prerequisites matured and eventually matured for a qualitatively new approach to the problems of war, peace and armies in the new historical conditions. Including for a qualitative Breakthrough in the main question of war, in its dialectics with politics, in its connections with classes and class interests, with humanity as a whole and the absolute interest in surviving. This Breakthrough was realized and took a central place in the new political thinking.

1.6. THE WORLD ON THE BORDER BETWEEN TWO MILLENNIA. THE PHILOSOPHY OF HISTORY, ON THE THRESHOLD OF A QUALITATIVELY NEW STAGE OF DEVELOPMENT.

The way this question is formulated can be met with the objection that preference has been given to too strong words, a qualitatively new stage, and in the development of such a fundamental science as philosophy. Yes, the words are indeed strong, but here are other words said about the current state of philosophical thought,,, Unfortunately, this great science, more than any other, has now moved away from the modern world". (See: Ligchev E. K., report to the all-Union conference with the heads of the departments of Social Sciences, October 1986). One of the most characteristic features of the new political thinking is that it far exceeds the problems of war and peace and its main ideas and historical role essentially extend to the main block of current problems of the philosophy of history. So it is not excluded that this thinking in its further development will impose itself precisely as a major new stage in the development of historical materialism, reflecting in itself the essence and laws of a long historical period, included within the framework of that social era that began with the victory of the Great October Socialist Revolution, and at the same time with very great specificity and relative independence, a period that is missing in the currently existing forecasts for future development of society. It is possible that this period will also acquire the character of an independent era. It is no coincidence that on the threshold of new political thinking the question arises: To what limit has the World reached in its development? And the natural continuation of this question, where is history heading, what else is destined for the peoples to experience, And what is subject to and beyond the control of man, and the impending fate on the border of two centuries.? The indomitable flow of history, writes Mikhail Gorbachev on this occasion, has already rushed towards the transition between the second and third millennium. What awaits us there, for this transition? From additional questions in this prelude to political thinking it becomes clear that a passionate appeal is addressed to today's humanity, to look soberly and realistically at the entire World Panorama, to free ourselves from the captivity of habitual schemes, to look at ourselves with new eyes. (See Mikhail Gorbachev, Perestroika and New Thinking, page 167). It is naive to think that the Question is addressed only to the West. Perhaps it is more logical to assume that the challenge hidden in this question is addressed primarily to the theory that claims a scientific approach to history, that is, to the state and tasks of Marxist-Leninist teaching. So, who should open their eyes, who should free themselves from dogmas and stereotypes, and what relation do these things have to the Philosophy of War, on the same historical border between the two centuries? For a philosophical analysis of social phenomena, this approach is of decisive importance, because it embodies in itself the Basic requirements of philosophical materialism, that thinking should reflect the realities of today, correspond to the state of social existence, resolutely break its connection with those concepts, views and doctrines in which, everything is fine, including in their completed axiomatic form, which suffers from only one drawback, that they no longer correspond to life, and are essentially a look at it, but with the eyes of the past. Unfortunately, this shortcoming is not foreign to the contemporary state of society and individual consciousness.

The best minds of humanity, Mikhail Gorbachev emphasizes, warned of the danger of our consciousness falling behind the rapid change of existence. This is especially urgent in our days. Man is already entering the galactic expanses. But, how many imperfect things still remain on earth. In a more concrete plan, the causes and social appearance of this contradiction between modern general human existence and historical consciousness of it are determined To a large extent, and perhaps to a decisive extent, by the clash between two basic, mutually opposing tendencies of development of the world as a whole. On the one hand, this is its deep contradiction, on the other, the increasing role of its integrity. Let us dwell in more detail on these two tendencies, because with their dialectical interaction with related the basic principles of new political thinking, and qualitative revolutionary changes in the Marxist-Leninist doctrine of war, peace and the army in modern conditions. The first tendency characterizes the multidimensionalityAnd deep opposition of the modern world. Having fallen primarily under the influence of two revolutions: the October 1917 revolution and the scientific and technical revolution, the world has changed beyond recognition. In every respect it is no longer what it was until recently, and at the same time it continues to change rapidly. Obviously, this is primarily about the existence of two powerful social systems, capitalism and socialism, and about hundreds of other small and large countries and peoples who are very actively looking for a path for their historical development. A kind of explosion of social orientation has resulted, which is polarized around the struggle between capitalism and socialism. A second significant moment in the action of the first trend is the colossal dimensions of the opposites of the modern historical process and the critical state of the contradictions from which this process is born. First of all, there are the two social systems and the growing confrontation between them, which on all levels, economic, political, ideological and military, has been going on for over 70 years, and under the theoretical aegis of the formula "who is who", which was declared the main contradiction of the era. But since this era,, has no end in sight,, and many predictions on this issue have been refuted by life, the question "who is who" has lost its connection with changes in social life and was subordinated to only one too indefinite criterion - the death of capitalism. However, when it became quite obvious that with this death of capitalism there arose a very real danger of another death of the entire human race, the formula who is who, turned into a mortal danger for political strategy. We can repeat a thousand times that it best expresses the main objective trends of modern world history, that it takes into account the class characteristics of the two social systems and the main contradiction of the era, that it is the logical historical continuation of Lenin's theory of the victory of the revolution in a separate country. But from these repetitions, nothing can change the fact that it was the historical escalation of "who is who" that brought things to such a critical limit beyond which there is no turning back. It brought them to the absurd. However, in order to avoid some misunderstandings, it is necessary to take into account two things: first, that the contradictions between socialism and capitalism from the victory of the October Revolution to the present day have changed their historical content on a huge scale.

And secondly, the attitude of capitalism and socialism to these contradictions was and remains fundamentally different. It was capitalism that immediately after the historical year of 1917 gave an ominous form to the question of who is who and is trying at all costs to wipe socialism off the face of the Earth. In many ways, this line is also characteristic of the political strategy of imperialism now, without understanding that in modern historical realities This is already complete absurdity. Having set off in the middle of the endlessly deepening confrontation, the world as a whole found itself facing several dead ends, threatening history with a global catastrophe. Nuclear street: ecological street: information street: street of rich and poor nations: maybe North-South: street of nuclear winter. Now the question is how history can stop its insane wandering from these roads and, secondly, how humanity can return to other, worthy of this century relations, before the irreparable has happened. It can be said without exaggeration that one of the most profound philosophical ideas of the 27th Congress of the Communist Party of the Soviet Union briefly played the role of an initial impetus to new political thinking. This is the statement: to make sense of the time in which we live in Lenin's way. That is, it is about a conscious rejection of some statements in which the meaning of history was reflected until yesterday, but today they are already the meaning of the past. Are they just myths, stereotypes, schemes and need to be rethought. Because it has been repeated thousands of times that the Marxist-Leninist teaching is not a dogma, it is a guide to action, and despite this, real threats have periodically been created that this Great Teaching will be imposed on the historical process as a dogma. This danger was taken into account in the warning of the 27th Party Congress: "Any attempt to turn the theory by which we are guided into a collection of rigid schemes and recipes, applicable everywhere and for all cases in life, most decisively contradicts the essence of Marxism-Leninism." (see Mikhail Gorbachev Political Report of the Central Committee of the Communist Party of the Soviet Union, to the 27th Congress of the Communist Party of the Soviet Union, page 5). Let us now see what the modern world is like and what its projection is in the new political thinking. In addition to the tendency that divides it, the development of this world has entered a period of the most complex alternatives and never before has it been subjected to such a strong political and physical strain. And the main factor that brought things to such a state is the prolonged preparation of humanity for waging war with modern means and, above all, with nuclear weapons. This process ended with a qualitative leap in the means of destruction, which for the first time in history has the man with the physical ability to destroy all life on planet Earth. When the first nuclear device was launched, the American physicist Professor Pendridge rightly exclaimed: "Now we are all scoundrels." The mastery of nuclear energy turned the 20th century into a great step towards the innermost secrets of nature. It makes earthly civilization comparable to the universe and reveals to humanity vast cosmic expanses for the mastery of which would be the most worthy crown of human reason. However, things did not go in this direction. The immense power over the mastered great natural force established militarism and with only 40 years of its domination humanity became a nuclear hostage.

It so happened that from the crown of reason "nuclear energy" with enormous speed and unsuspected diligence a tragic Crown of History was prepared. Who is to blame for this terrible state of affairs? Who was pushing the world, with some demonic force, to the very edge of absurdity? On the one hand, as an answer to this question, the concept of red militarism and Soviet, military danger took precedence over everything, and on the other, as the core of the ideological position of socialism, the thesis was raised that socialism does not need wars to assert itself in history, and that the blame lies entirely with capitalism. Many books have been written about this dispute. And the truth cannot remain hidden forever from those millions of people in capitalist countries, in which a fear psychosis is created by Soviet tanks, missiles, submarines. The films America and Rambo will be re-released, and new ones like them will be created, but this world, including the American one, will eventually understand that the Soviet peoples do not threaten anyone with anything, that the successful construction of socialism requires not armament and war, but peace and the rational use of material resources and wealth for the ever-more complete satisfaction of material and spiritual needs and the multifaceted development of people in this society. However, it seems that these words did not reach the billionaires. And even if they did, they had no interest in believing them. Interest! Here is the focus that explains why, despite all the facts of real history, anti-Sovietism has become not only the lie of the century, but is a cancer of the Spiritual Forces and culture of the West and, what is worst of all, an ideological blessing - ideological incitement to militarism. For example, it is possible and correct to defend the dialectical-materialist point of view that the enormous zig-zag that modern history is making cannot be explained by the determining role of psychic phenomena. No matter how powerful the modern industry of lies is, no matter how much effort the ideological and information empires of capitalism make, no matter what concepts are hatched in the places of bourgeois ideology, they still cannot be and are not the first cause of the unprecedented militarization that has engulfed the capitalist countries, and above all the USA and its NATO allies. For example, the fact that currently over 60 million people are still engaged in military production, and that about 25% of scientists from all over the world - that is over 500 thousand people - are putting their talent on the altar of the death of man and humanity cannot be explained either by the bestial nature of human instincts, or by the mind-boggling state of anti-communism and anti-Sovietism, or by the colossal ignorance of those teachers from the Federal Republic of Germany who have instilled in their students one of the most modern libels of anti-Sovietism - better Star Wars than a colony of Moscow. We say these things not to justify the ideology and the ideologists of militarism. On the contrary, by taking on the role of instigators and arsonists, they take upon themselves the greatest guilt that can ever exist in the thousand-year history of mankind. This is the guilt and responsibility for the survival of civilization, and it can be assumed that a significant part of yesterday's and today's servants of militarism will wake up from the nightmare and will also look at the world with open eyes to understand that the matter is no longer about communism or capitalism, but about what unites them into one whole and is called humanity.

Once upon a time, Karl Marx and Friedrich Engels rightly criticized the abstract approach to this word, but modern history has filled it not just with new, but with fateful content. Thus we come to the fundamental idea, we would call the idea of ideas, of an evolutionary in modern conditions, most accurate conceptual subjective reflection of the state of history and the most realistic program for the cohesion and action of peoples. This is the idea of the integrity, interconnectedness, of the unity of the human race. Now, if not critics, then at least doubts about the class essence of this concept will certainly appear. But before we doubt a priori, as they say, or on the theoretical basis of well-learned formulas about classes and class struggle, it is necessary to put things on the plane on which they actually are, that is, to take into account historical realities.

The confrontation between the two social systems has reached such a level that its further intensification becomes impossible. Now, very quickly, from the scales of the confrontation, a new and wise planetary consciousness is being formed, which increasingly understands the turning point of world history and the enormous danger that the worst may happen to it at any moment. What to do next? To intensify the confrontation? But this is simply impossible! To intensify the military-technical confrontation, that is, the arms race? This is also pointless and insane. To increase ideological tension, to give food to its monsters, anti-humanism, racism, nationalism, chauvinism, anti-communism, anti-Sovietism and all other antis and isms that play a significant role in the confrontation of an already divided world to the limit? And this should not be done, because it is also aimed at the general destruction of humanity.

Wherever the realities of the modern world are observed, it reveals to the philosophical mind of humanity a sharp, both mature and immature, objective need for unity and integrity, capable of overcoming the severe consequences of the confrontations of the 20th century. This is precisely what is meant by one of the main philosophical ideas of the new political thinking - about the priority in modern conditions of universal human values.

Mikhail Gorbachev writes: "We have made our choice... To ignore what divides us, for the sake of common human interests, for the sake of life on earth." and further: "Humanity must recognize the vital necessity of the priority of common humanity, as the main imperative of the era." (see: Mikhail Gorbachev "Perestroika and New Thinking for Our Country and for the Whole World." S. 1987, page 172.)

It is still difficult to assess how this imperative of the times is being met by the main social forces of modernity. But it was natural to expect that its unusualness compared to the heavy and super-heavy class and confrontations of recent times would inevitably provoke very different ideological resonances, from relief and hope from some, to disbelief and open hostility from others. And indeed, that is exactly what happened.

The most reactionary supporters of the power policy towards socialism characterized this thesis as an ideological maneuver and a lure of Moscow, dictated by the difficulties in the development of the socialist countries, and called on the West to preserve its traditional attitude towards socialism. Strange as it may sound, but a similar reaction was also made by some dogmatically inclined ideologists of socialism, who saw in the new political thinking an encroachment on principles, a shaking of the logic of socialism and almost a revisionist rejection of the class tradition of Marxism-Leninism. It is logical to assume that these contradictory ideological assessments of the new political thinking will be preserved and will create certain difficulties in its consolidation in the consciousness and in the political life of the peoples. But it is even more logical to assert that the objective historical process is powerfully entering a long period during which not just any, but fateful universal human values will stand above everything else, including class tendencies in its development. Not by the power of thinking, but in the objective reality itself, a new profound revolutionary coup is taking place, towards a qualitatively new dialectic, the core of which is the priority role of universal human values. Thinking only reflects these processes, and may differ from the objective state of affairs, but best of all if it truthfully reflects the trends of development. This is precisely where the strength and advantages of new political thinking over all other points of view lie. It is the modern, common to all ideological platform for the unity of peoples in solving extremely difficult social problems affecting the destinies of all humanity. The core of a given concept emits a powerful and determining priority methodological function, which plays a leading role in the approach to all other problems, issues and aspects of the concept itself. And in our case, with the new political thinking, there are as many questions as we want. Here is a part of them: the problem of the main contradiction of the era, in the Light of the priority of the human beginning, the theory of classes and class struggle and the place of the World Socialist Community in it, the problem of the content of the new period in development, into which the historical era of transition from capitalism to socialism is entering, the dialectics not only of the universal and class, but also of the national and international, of revolutionary movements and social revolutions, taken in relation to the unity of the world, the problem of the way in which one of the basic laws of the development of history, the Law of the decisive role of the People's Masses, will be realized in the future, not to mention war and its interaction with all philosophical and non-philosophical questions of historical development and the participation of opposing ideologies in the new approach to the future of humanity.

It can definitely be said that in the general system of these issues, the modern objective need to elevate the limited understanding of class and national interests over ideological and other differences has acquired increasing priority importance. All social systems today are and can be rivals in the struggle for ideas, but their partnership in the struggle to preserve life on earth has acquired the character of a categorical imperative.

In close connection with the priority of the universal human principle, the question of the social characteristics of the peaceful coexistence of capitalism and socialism also received a fundamentally new solution.

It must be frankly admitted that the statement in the new program of the Communist Party of the Soviet Union that the complex relations between the two social systems are not a form of class struggle and that relations between countries with different social systems must be ideologized sounded almost sensational. This issue will probably still be developed in a philosophical and methodological plan, while at the same time efforts will increase to bring the real relations between the two social systems out of the difficult state of class confrontation and to deeply restructure them in the direction of equality, cooperation, mutual economic, ecological, scientific, technical and other benefits, and a number of other things that are worthy of relations between civilized peoples, countries and states. This is also not an illusion for two reasons: first, because it was the class confrontation that brought things to their current disastrous state, and second, these relations of a fundamentally new nature are not only desirable, but also objectively necessary. In this case, however, the fact that there is a fundamental difference between the relations in a state where a given minority exploits and oppresses the masses of the people on the economic basis of private ownership of the means of production, and the relations between the same social-class groups, but without the presence of exploitation and oppression, when they are separated in a state relationship, plays a primary role. In the first case, class struggle is inevitable, but it also has many changes in its forms, and does not always develop into armed struggle. And even then, when the latter becomes inevitable, its material preparation and conduct are quite noticeably different from a world war. And one more thing, every war between states, unlike civil ones, in a rather complex way involves national interests, and in essence it is the national, related to state borders, territories, threatened national freedom, national interests, and others, that is the main form of manifestation of military confrontation.

However, when interstate relations are subordinated to the idea of class struggle, things naturally begin to develop in the direction that has been dominant over the past 70 years. And if this process ("God forbid") develops in these material conditions that are typical of the 20th century, including the presence of controlled nuclear energy, nothing else can result at the end of this process, except what has been achieved: endless mutual distrust, typical of class relations, and an ever-increasing readiness "to destroy the enemy", or "to deal a crushing counter-blow to the enemy".

Subjected to this bilateral formula, interstate relations not only lost their normal content, but reached the point of absurdity, where only one perspective remained, **mutual multiple destruction** , no longer devoid of any class or any other goal.

Any attempt to separate these two processes, the disastrous one that brought history to the brink of self-destruction, from the theory of class struggle, almost as the main regulator of interstate relations, after the victory of the Great October Socialist Revolution, means once again ignoring the truth, which, incidentally, quite often accompanied the construction of socialism, as soon as it became necessary at the 27th Congress of the Communist Party of the Soviet Union to emphasize that the first lesson that should form the basis of perestroika is the lesson of truth.

It is now clear that the continued treatment of peaceful coexistence as a form of class struggle has nothing to do with the struggle for social progress and does not meet the needs of the time at the end of the 20th century.

However, it should be further clarified when and under what circumstances this concept was adopted and to what extent Lenin's concepts of peaceful coexistence differ from it. It is not excluded that it will turn out to be a kind of surrogate for the Trotskyist leftist concept of the "permanent" Revolution in the Soviet Union, as its state bridgehead. In general, the further development of the new political thinking will inevitably be accompanied by quite serious reflection on the Philosophy of building a classless society, both in its internal aspects and as a world historical process.

Of course, these are complex questions related to the most fundamental theoretical propositions of historical materialism. And it is no coincidence that Mikhail Gorbachev considers it necessary to emphasize that **"to some it may seem strange that the communists emphasize universal human interests and values"** (see Mikhail Gorbachev. "Perestroika and New Thinking". page 182).

Actually, it's an understatement to say "strange." After all, until a few years ago, this thesis would have been immediately assessed as a "revision" of Marxism-Leninism, and its author would have increased the number of victims.

This is what used to happen to anyone who allowed themselves to look at some issues differently than the imposed standard, and it was in this way that "creative thought was expelled from social science, and superficial, voluntaristic assessments and judgments became indisputable truths, only for comment. (see Mikhail Gorbachev "Perestroika and New Thinking". page 21).

And in the same way, it was they, the social sciences, that "suffered the most from the cult of personality, from bureaucratic methods of leadership, from dogmatism and incompetent intervention" (see Mikhail Gorbachev. "With Lenin's Wisdom and Responsibility." 1988, page 553).

But the reverse side of this problem is no less fundamentally important. Pluralism of views, discussions, freedom of thought, publicity, including on some of the most fundamental issues of the dialectics of the restructuring of the modern world, will inevitably clash, will enter into dialogue and struggle with those who are unacceptable, grossly hostile to socialism, revisionist, dogmatic bourgeois, bourgeois-liberal, and others. And here In this connection, a true reference point and criterion of the movement towards truth are needed. And there is no better reference point in this regard than the interests of socialism and man and there cannot be. "We - writes Mikhail Gorbachev on this occasion - affirm the pluralism of opinions and reject the spiritual monopoly. But in everything we must proceed from the person, from the interests of the people, to affirm the humane values of socialism. Then a clean and normal working atmosphere in society and intense work of creative thought, and a true flowering of culture will be ensured." There is nothing else to add to this except the popular "May God grant it."

Two more considerations are of paramount importance for the correct attitude to the core of the new thinking. The first concerns the one-sided understanding of the class approach, the underestimation, and in many cases the misunderstanding of the organic connection between the historical mission of the working class and the universal ideals of social development. The deepest meaning, which also defines the humanism of the proletarian revolutionary cause, is that it is not this or that class, not this or that people, but all of humanity that is to be liberated. Through the prism of this meaning , **the class approach is only a means of realizing universal ideals** , which defines the latter as higher than class values and interests. In this regard, let us not forget Vladimir

Ilyich Lenin, who wrote:

" From the point of view of the fundamental question of Marxism, the interests of social development stand higher than the interests of the proletariat."

For too long, this fundamental aspect of Marxism has been sacrificed on the altar of the "proletarian point of view." And why has this happened? Perhaps out of fear of making common cause with the enemies of the working class.

The second consideration concerns the way of understanding the contradiction between the class and the universal, the limits within which this contradiction increases or decreases, and the conditions under which they are forced to exchange places in the historical process.

In fact, the theory only elaborated on that distant historical period when, after the complete victory of communism, **the proletarian point of view would fall away to be replaced by the point of view of man as a generic being, when the actual individual subject - in the words of Karl Marx - would perceive within himself the abstract citizen of the state, and in his individual relations would become a generic being** , that is, when both a class and a socially homogeneous society would be built.

The problem is that in its thousand-year history, man has not had much opportunity to feel like a generic being. On the contrary, generations after generations have built their individual relationships as anti-generic beings, that is, on the basis of what alienates and distinguishes them, not what unites them. For example, the worker is defined as anti-capitalist, the capitalist as anti-worker. Even in their inter-national relations, peoples have been forced to assert themselves in the same way: for example, the Bulgarian is defined by centuries-old struggle against aggressive neighboring peoples, states and countries and, vice versa.

And now, at the end of the twentieth century, somehow suddenly and unexpectedly the idea of the priority of the universal in a world divided to the extreme by class, national and other contradictions and conflicts!!

Perhaps the great remoteness of this task in the future, affecting its realization on an international, or rather global, level, has created a psychological attitude not to expect any significant changes in the relationship between the universal and the class in the dialectics of the historical process in the near future.

However, the main role here was played by the dialectics of objective circumstances after the victory of the Great October Socialist Revolution. The point is that World Capitalism reacted to this fact precisely as a World Class Force and throughout the entire period acted towards the homeland of socialism from a class position of force.

Socialism was virtually deprived of the opportunity to put into practice those principles of peaceful coexistence that Vladimir Ilyich Lenin had developed. Moreover, there was no political experience of rationally building relations between countries with different social systems. Since 1917, the entire policy of World Imperialism has turned into a sinister anti-socialist chain. The military intervention in the first years of Soviet power was an aggression not against Russia, but against the newly born socialism in Russia. The economic blockades, diplomatic boycotts and sanitary cordons that followed were also carried out on a deep class basis. What fascism - the striking force of imperialism - had to do was also not anti-socialist, but super-anti-socialist in nature, and more precisely, "to wipe socialism off the face of the Earth."

The post-war Cold War also began, also on a deep class basis. And it was during these dark years that the sinister relay race of several specific plans by NATO and the Pentagon for a nuclear attack on the USSR and the countries of the socialist community developed. And again with the aim of burying socialism. The nuclear bombs over Hiroshima and Nagasaki became a warning to socialism, at the cost of 400 thousand innocent victims. And during the same four post-war decades, which means that funds worth $ 150 are taken from every inhabitant of the earth, military budgets have acquired astronomical dimensions, and by 1986 armaments were absorbing one and a half million dollars every minute, 90 million dollars every hour, about 2.2 billion dollars every day, and over 800 billion dollars every year, which means that funds worth $ 150 are taken from every inhabitant of the earth annually. Part of these billions went to replace the cordon sanitaire with a cordon of military bases, numbering over 1,500, scattered across the territory of about 40 countries. "Sovereign" ones at that! Even more difficult years followed with the deployment of cruise missiles on European territory, the development of scenarios for victorious wars with limited use of nuclear weapons, and finally the turn of the notorious "SOI", for which it is planned to build 10 combat space orbital stations in geostationary orbits by 1995, and another 10 in the next 25 years, which will cost over 2 trillion dollars.

The long-awaited stealth aircraft, the Stealth retaliation aircraft, which cost over $2 billion to develop, has already been shown.

And all this is done in honor of socialism, for historical revenge and for world domination. It is in this situation that the military danger has become a constant factor for socialism.

And during this same time, Golden Times came for the military-industrial complex. Who could have expected production with a 2000% profit?

And yet during the same time, Reagan, almost in the form of inappropriate humor, addressed the American people with the words: "America prays to God for peace, but the Evil Empire, the Soviet Union, is rapidly creating a mortal danger to the free world."

We have reason to ask: to which god does the president pray? Isn't it the one with the two thousand percent, about whom Marx said back in the last century that he comes to life like a vampire as soon as he gets the opportunity to suck living human labor, that his vampiric essence is proportional to the percentage of profit, and at 300% profit, he is ready to commit any crime, even if the noose of the gallows hangs over his head? Isn't it this God who, following the example of the ancient pagan idol, loved to drink nectar only from the skulls of murdered people, and in modern conditions, from the murder of all humanity?

In general, the main thing in world history after 1917 is the constantly deepening class conflict, in which imperialism knew its goal and did not choose its means for its realization. In the end, it fell into a disastrous state of "Sovietphobia."

Now, when it comes to the priority of the universal over the class, the point is not to question the class nature of the clashes between the two social systems during the past period. And today this approach fully corresponds to the class society in which class interests are opposed, and to the realities of International life also permeated by this opposition. (See Mikhail Gorbachev. "Perestroika and New Political Thinking." Page 182). The point is something else, to understand that as a historical process this class confrontation has reached such a point beyond which its further escalation is impossible, because it leads to the self-destruction of the human race, and even to life on the planet, to its transformation into a lifeless cosmic body.

To understand that now that weapons of mass destruction have appeared, an objective limitation has appeared for class confrontation on the International Arena. This is a threat of total destruction.

And what to do in this state of affairs? Nothing but politics and thinking that seek new paths for history, because the old paths lead to its last day.

If there are still any doubts about the possibilities of such a policy, let us bear in mind that this is a completely new state of human history, which must be understood only in one version, the one that is characteristic of the new thinking, because objectively speaking, there is no other reasonable or approximately reasonable alternative. For the other direction, Einstein's bitter maxim remains: if people still destroy each other, the Universe will not shed a single Elsa for it. Of paramount importance is also the question of the terms for the practical political realization of the new thinking. The possibilities for this process to drag on in time are very limited. History makes us hurry... Tomorrow it may be too late. And the next day we may not be here at all. (See Mikhail Gorbachev. Perestroika and the New Political Thinking. page 182). Particularly dangerous in this regard may also be numerous coincidences of a different nature, which from a philosophical point of view. It means that the future of enlightened humanity of the 20th century is becoming something like a toy in the hands of fate, in captivity of technology and military technocratic logic. It is this circumstance that gives an increasingly critical importance to the time factor. **It is no coincidence that in his remarkable declaration of February 15, 1986, Mikhail Gorbachev raised the extremely bold program for humanity to put away its nuclear swords and shields and destroy them by the end of the century!**

1.7. THE END OF THE CENTURIES-OLD RELATIONSHIP "POLITICS - WAR". THE NUCLEAR IMPERATIVE OF POLITICS.

Is the connection between war and politics genetic?
Clausewitz or Lenin - Why is historical truth distorted?

We have already set forth the basic, let us call them conditionally, classical Marxist-Leninist propositions, concerning the dialectics of war and politics. Moreover, it was necessary to explicitly emphasize that we are talking not only and not so much about the German military theorist Clausewitz, but about a number of sufficiently clear and categorical statements by Vladimir Ilyich Lenin that war is a continuation of politics by other violent means. On the basis of this theoretical statement, a comprehensive attitude to the essence, character and factors on which each specific war depends was formed.

For years, certain reservations have arisen about the truth of this statement when its methodological function is applied not to just any war, but to the most sinister for the fate of humanity, the nuclear missile war.

In the interest of truth, it is necessary to point out that serious objections to the applicability of Clausewitz's view to nuclear war were raised by some bourgeois scholars a long time ago. Particularly typical in this regard is the case of John Kingston MacLeary, who wrote as early as the 1950s:

"If before war was a tool of State policy... Now, total war can become a tool for the destruction of all warring states and civilizations...

In the event of war, nothing would be further from the truth than Clausewitz's famous statement that war is the continuation of politics by other means. Such a war... would mean the end of politics and complete mutual extermination."

It is difficult to find a difference between the given point of view and the statements of the new political thinking. But, in that not so distant time, such views were immediately, almost a priori, given the well-known label "bourgeois", and any attempt to seek a more precise solution to this question, more adequate to the new military historical realities, was met with a knife by self-proclaimed "major specialists", for whom the main argument remained invariably the same - the name of Vladimir Ilyich Lenin. It even reached such a paradox that the point of view "war is a continuation of politics..." was elevated into a kind of ideological cult, and was declared the main dividing line between the Marxist-Leninist doctrine of war and peace, on the one hand, and bourgeois views, on the other.

And because it is not so pleasant to be called an "anti-Leninist" (I have experienced it myself) and along with losing some small things in your life before you perish in a nuclear war, the search for truth was directed again within the same formula with the comforting addition that "nuclear war is very specific" (see. Global Strategy. Moscow. 1959. Page 290.).

This is how one of the most rigid dogmas in the Marxist-Leninist doctrine of war and peace, about the impossibility of breaking the connection between war and politics, was formed. Even the inevitable destruction of politics itself in a nuclear war turned out to be an insufficient argument for reconsidering and possibly changing the thesis of the past. And when the idea appeared in the system of new political thinking that in a missile-nuclear war the connection between war and politics was broken, attempts were made to save the old formula through the theory of the "double truth" - one for us, the other for the enemy. Several years passed and it became quite obvious that this issue was far more serious than some political game. Moreover - this issue was fateful!

It is no coincidence that it is emphasized that the main starting principle of the new political thinking is that nuclear war cannot be a means of achieving political, economic, ideological, or any goals, and immediately after that another equally extremely important statement, referring to the depth of the revolutionary changes in the Marxist-Leninist Philosophy of War: this conclusion has a truly revolutionary character, because it means a radical break with traditional ideas about war and peace. (See Mikhail Gorbachev. "Perestroika and the New Thinking:... Page 174).

So, when it comes to theoretical propositions, with the help of which the essence of war is revealed, not just anything, we will cite verbatim those new propositions that were embedded in the new thinking as its basic principle. And this is very important for the methodological approach to military phenomena.

"Clausewitz's formula that war is a continuation of politics, only by other means... is hopelessly outdated. Its place is in libraries." (see Mikhail Gorbachev. "Perestroika and New Thinking...", page 174).

And immediately after that, as a fundamental principle of the new political thinking, the thesis was raised that there can be no winners in a nuclear war, that such a war cannot be used as a means to achieve any political goals, from which it logically follows that the connection with politics has also been severed. All this is perfectly correct and has acquired the status of a nuclear imperative in relation to politics.

It is not clear, however, why only Clausewitz is being discussed now? For anyone who is at all familiar with this issue, such an approach is unacceptable and too much like a silent and unnecessary curtsy to Vladimir Ilyich Lenin.

First, it is unacceptable to pass over in silence the high assessment that Vladimir Ilyich Lenin gave to Clausewitz at the time, referring him to the most famous writers on the Philosophy of War. Second, it is even more unacceptable to pass over in silence Lenin's personal attitude to the dialectic of war with politics. He not only accepts Clausewitz's point of view, explicitly emphasizing that such was always the point of view of Marx and Engels..., but he extensively develops this point of view, relating it both to the politics of the bourgeoisie, in the conditions of the First World War, and to the politics of the working class, to the revolution and the Peace, to classes and political parties, to small and large nations, and so on.

Of particular importance in this case is the fact that Lenin repeatedly returned to this question during the years of the First World War, when the objective conditions themselves required the working class in the belligerent capitalist countries to have its own political attitude to the war. And in these conditions, and also in the even more destructive Second World War, the fighting of multimillion-strong armies on the territory of several continents was carried out under the sign of strict political goals, that is, they were a continuation and means of the corresponding policy. All this remains valid for the wars from up to the Nuclear Period. But when in the development of military affairs nuclear weapons appeared and became not a dominant, but, more precisely, an absolute factor, it is quite natural, completely in the spirit of dialectics to take into account this Typical transformation of opposites into each other - from one point of view to make a transition to another, diametrically opposite. Because the meaning of the points of view is not in who and when they were defended, but in their adequacy to historical realities.

In some authors, the ideas of the new political thinking are associated with Lenin's statement to Nadezhda Krupskaya, an assumption that when an absolute weapon is created, war will become impossible. Such a connection can be accepted, but only in the most general terms. As for what actually happened, with the emergence and colossal accumulation of nuclear weapons, and for a perfectly short historical period, it is more logical to assume that even Lenin's genius could not have allowed such a tragic and dangerous combination of circumstances, threatening all of humanity and life on the planet with universal destruction. As a danger, nuclear war is an absolute Unique that cannot be described with the additional help of categories. More specific guesses about the peculiarities and specificity of the unique nature of the nuclear guillotine are found in the manifesto of B. Russell and Albert Einstein from the 1950s, in which they explicitly emphasized that nuclear energy introduces humanity into a new era, where the concepts of enemy, victory and the like are not at all suitable for communication between nations. A manifesto that ends with an appeal to all people: "remember your belonging to the human race and forget everything else". Only 30 years later it became clear that in a global nuclear conflict there will be neither winners nor losers, but the entire civilization will inevitably perish.

And it is quite fair in the light of this scenario to characterize such a war as meaningless and irrational, because in the past, wars have been given some meaning by the idea of just or unjust political goals.

Now this connection has completely broken down, which means this war is becoming meaningless.

Here, however, it is necessary to protect the philosophical-methodological analysis of this question from mixing it with other questions. For example, with the question, From what womb was this danger born and grew? When and how did this happen? In the new political thinking, a large place is devoted to the aggressive policy of imperialism, which, without taking into account the realities, for quite a long time was, (And this is still the case now), striving like some blind force, to necessarily acquire military superiority over socialism and then to go to historical revenge for the defeats it suffered in the past. Instead, however, a military-strategic parity was obtained and the impossibility of further applying a policy of force against socialism, or of violating this parity. This is how the peoples and systems really resembled climbers tied with one rope, or people in one boat, who can only perish together or survive together. And with the addition that if the worst happens, there will be no second Noah's Ark!

It is even scary to think about what is still to come. But in reality it exists: first, as a technical possibility, second, as the thinking of imperialism from the "Stone Age", which turned anti-Sovietism into its main profession, third, as a monster called militarism, fourth, as a force policy, fifth, as a weakened moral immune system that cannot understand the dialectics of war and universal human moral values, sixth, as the first atomic sin committed, called Hiroshima. But all this not only does not support the old formula of the relationship between politics and war, but on the contrary, is evidence that this relationship has already been broken and in a missile-nuclear war it is impossible for them to be united as a goal and means, including in a limited nuclear war, and even in wars with modern classical means.

The highly discursive environment in which the transition to a qualitatively new position on the dialectic of war with politics was taking place requires additional analysis of some of the aspects of this issue, and especially those that could still be used as arguments in favor of the already old point of view.

Conditionally, these aspects can be divided into several groups: epistemological and basic, technical and military, national, state, regional and global, and others. Depending on the problem of interest to us, the grouping can be done in another way. In this case, this is not the most important thing. The main thing is that these aspects are real sides of the dialectic between war and politics for two reasons: first, because every war affects society as a whole, and second, because the same thing applies to politics. For example, every war depends on the mode of production and, in turn, has a powerful reverse effect on it. Every war affects peoples and classes, states and social systems, regions, and now the planet as a whole.

War transforms the social energy of ideas into a material force of destruction. Including when, nevertheless, some political goals are achieved with its help. Including when these goals are just.

It is precisely this basic feature of war, the fact that it falls on people as a particularly evil and unbearable force, that explains to us the colossal tension that accompanies the transition from politics to a given war. A serious mistake is made when one does not understand or obscures the fact that war as a continuation of politics in the classical definition is nothing other than the transition of an entire society from a state of peace and life to a state of war, savagery, death!

How is the situation with politics? In much the same way as war.

It is incorrect to consider it only as some level in the structure of society, next to which are located, some above, others below, on some other levels. Rather, it is that center that expresses the will of the whole society. If it is class, it is natural that this will should also be class.

But even the most class society is not able to create an absolutely anti-social policy. This policy will always have some logic in its political goals. Logic itself can in no way be formed only in the bosom of politics. Rather, there it can be violated, undergoing some unexpected deformations of a subjectivist nature. Socialism also does not have historical insurance against such anti-logic, as evidenced by the deformations associated with the so-called Cult of Personality.

Politics is not simply a concentrated expression of economics. It is a concentrated expression of interests from the base to the top of society. At the same time, a concentration of diverse and extremely contradictory interests, in which the economic ones play a leading role, and the overall, not only economic, interests of the class in power play a dominant role.

And this policy, at a given moment, is Authorized to translate society into a state of war and in the new conditions to function as a military policy itself. What does this mean, Authorized? In the direct sense, this means that it expresses the will and interests of society, but even when this is not the case, when politics is, as they say, adventurous and is directed towards goals that are unfeasible and alien to the people, even in this case the decisions it makes concern the whole of society and therefore these decisions are burdened by the fate of the peoples as a whole. It is this connection of politics with the whole of society that gives its decisions to enter war a fateful character. It is quite obvious that when a policy "crosses its Rubicon", and goes to war, it, this policy, experiences the braking effect of numerous and very different factors on itself.

If the constraints are too strong, it may not cross the border towards war at all. What is this in that case? Again, a policy that has been abandoned for some reason, or has been diverted by some factors from the continuation of war, that is, it remains a peaceful policy.

Restrainers and Stimulators. Here is the great question of the dialectical transition from the politics of Peace to the politics of War. There is no doubt that interests stand behind both, but only in the end, only as the final result of a torturous process to which essentially the whole of society is subjected and which becomes even more torturous with the outbreak of war.

In a concise form, what has been said above can be reduced to the following: the ease with which the words "war is a continuation of politics" are uttered is generally incommensurable with the colossal difficulties of the actual entry of society into a state of war. Even in older historical conditions, when politics did not have to play the role of Hamlet, it was very often forced to abandon war as its own continuation.

It is very important in this case to take into account some other considerations. The first of them concerns the relationship of interests with war. Indeed, it is this relationship that determines the position of politics towards war. They push it in this direction, but not in the absolute sense of the word. The problem is that, in relation to interests, war is always a risk factor towards them, including those interests that at a given moment are pushing politics towards war with the greatest force.

And when some lovers of strong phrases ask themselves Where

does war come from? From heaven or from earth? They should be answered: from the special state of contradictions First of all, in the economic basis of antagonistic socio-economic formations. Here and nowhere else is the so-called genetic, let us also call it the primary, objective, and necessary cause of wars in general. But this cause brings into active condition a very large number of other factors, already of a political, ideological and moral nature, which also make their contribution to the movement of things towards the fateful decisions to wage war, that is, they exert a secondary determining influence on these processes.

And to all this should be added the personal subjective moment of the currently active leading political parties and their leaders. Because it is not without importance who, in a given set of contradictions and circumstances, will make the decision to wage war: conservative republicans or National Socialists, Napoleon, Bismarck, Hitler or some other person.

Taking into account the entire set of circumstances and reasons that underlie the transition from politics to war, we come to the only correct conclusion that this process is highly contradictory and that not only the factors of peace, but also the factors of war contain within themselves certain hesitations, problems, and contradictions regarding the question of whether or not to start a given war.

In short, decisions to wage war, not in the symbolic sense, but in the literal sense, are truly the most fateful decisions in the lives not only of nations, but also of those classes and political forces that have some interest in war.

How are things in modern conditions? We will answer with words, some of which we have already quoted on another occasion: now, when weapons of mass (general!) destruction are being made, an objective limitation has appeared for the class confrontation on the International Arena. This is the threat of general destruction. For the first time, a real, not speculative, present, not future, universal human interest arises to save civilization from catastrophe.

This is this contemporary universal human interest, which confronts all other mutually contradictory interests, and in such forms that have no other alternative, neither class nor national, nor religious nor regional, that is, an interest of an imperative nature.

A significant role in this case is also played by the emerging military-strategic Parity and the impossibility of its unilateral violation. Some authors have called this state of affairs a "nuclear stalemate", but it seems that the definition "equilibrium of death" is preferable, because unlike the chess position called stalemate, equilibrium can at any moment turn into a Universal tragedy.

In his remarkable speech to the 43rd session of the United Nations General Assembly, Mikhail Gorbachev again returned to this issue and explicitly emphasized that nuclear weapons are a material symbol of absolute military power that has reached the absolute limits of its self-development. This power cannot be used unilaterally from the standpoint of any limited interests, which means that it somehow rises above politics and any attempt to put it at the service of any policy turns the latter into an absurd activity, into an absurd policy. Unfortunately, in the capitalist countries there are still strong reactionary, in fact super-reactionary circles that still maintain the inertia of confrontation with socialism and cannot understand how senseless and dangerous this military-political position is in modern historical realities.

Along with the connection between war and politics, nuclear weapons have severed two other traditional millennia-old connections: first, between power and security, and second, between war and progress (revolution).

For centuries, power and its growth have been a kind of guarantor of security, and for centuries it was on this principle that the main problems of the security of nations were solved. Now, in this directive, we have a typical case of the reversal of opposites. Any attempt to unilaterally strengthen security leads to destabilization and an increase in general insecurity.

And the logic of this new dialectic is contained in the critical values of security and uncertainty contained in the new weapons systems. Security is indivisible! It can only be the same or not exist at all. (See Mikhail Gorbachev..., Perestroika and New Thinking. page 176). The situation is similar with the connection of war with revolution. Progress in modern conditions can in no way be tied to the outcome of a missile-nuclear war. This situation can become a starting point. For serious reflection And about the possible nature of nuclear war. By what criteria could it, for example, be characterized for some as just, and for others as unjust, Since it leads in both cases to the same result - the destruction of civilization.

As we see, the new political thinking is indeed characterized by profound qualitative changes in the Philosophy of War and Peace. So profound that it can safely be considered as a historically new stage in the development of the Marxist-Leninist doctrine of war, peace and the army, which has yet to be realized in world historical practice, including in military affairs.

And this new stage is in a deep and inextricable methodological connection with the acute contemporary need for a qualitative renewal of the fundamental propositions of historical materialism.

Because even now very serious methodological contradictions are noticeable between the Philosophy of War and Peace in the new political thinking, and the still dominant philosophical views on such cardinal issues of our time as the question of the main contradiction of the era, presented in the ominous formula who-who, about the two modern socio-economic formations and the overly simplified ideas about the struggle between them, about the correlation and dialectics of universal and class values, and the obvious absolutization of the class approach. Referred to the Philosophy of War and Peace, these positions play the role of a kind of methodological brake on new ideas. Obviously, the Marxist-Leninist philosophy of history is also faced with the great question: to look at the world with new eyes, and if this world enters a new, unexpected, unusual, historical era, philosophy has nothing left but to embark on the path of adequate deep internal changes. And this need is now so acute that we could safely call it a philosophical-methodological imperative at the time.

2. NEW POLITICAL THINKING AND SOME CURRENT PHILOSOPHICAL AND METHODOLOGICAL PROBLEMS OF MILITARY THEORY AND PRACTICE. A RADICAL BREAK WITH TRADITIONAL IDEAS ABOUT WAR AND PEACE

2.1. For a new approach to philosophical and methodological problems of military phenomena at the contemporary stage.

From the fact that the struggle for the survival of mankind is entering a decisive stage, the problems of the military defense of socialism in no way lose their importance. On the contrary! It should not be forgotten that the chances of peace are connected with the historical role of the so-called military-strategic parity that the socialist countries have achieved, and that its maintenance is a primary task of the armed forces of socialism. Secondly, it is not easy to predict to what extent and how the forces of imperialism will be curbed, one of the central questions of the new political thinking without underestimating the historical role of Reykjavik and the treaty on the reduction of two classes of missiles. It is difficult to assume that the dismantling of the mountains of weapons and the cessation of armaments will develop without contradictions and desperate resistance of the forces of war. It is more likely that these forces will retreat if this happens at all, as they say, with a fight, to maneuver, and under certain circumstances even to attack the forces of peace. An example in this regard is the reluctance to stop the implementation of the Strategic Defense Initiative (SDI), despite the great instability it could create in international security, as well as the state of military budgets in capitalist countries. (See: "The Race for Armed NATO Countries". Moscow. Zapetayka 1988. "Militarism. Figures and Facts." Moscow 1985.)

Concerns in this regard are also numerous reports of new NATO rearmament. What does it mean, for example, that in Western Europe preparations are being made to replace the Lance missiles with a range of up to 130 km with a qualitatively new missile with a range of up to 500 km, or to modernize air-to-ground missiles and nuclear ammunition for various artillery systems? These and many other facts are what the Chief of the General Staff of the Armed Forces of the Union of Soviet Socialist Republics, Army General Moisey Moiseyev, has in mind, writing that the condemnation of nuclear war in the political vocabulary and military doctrines of the West is nothing more than a declaration to reassure the public. (See: Moiseyev. The Soviet Military Doctrine: Implementing Its Defensive Orientation. People's Army, March 21, 1989.)

Regardless of everything, however, it is deeply wrong to think that, given the availability of this data, the penetration of the ideas of new political thinking into the armed forces of socialism could cause manifestations of abstract pacifism, detached from military realities, and ultimately a weakening of the defense capability of socialism.

The danger of the illusions of pacifism and its negative consequences in the training of troops really exists. It is not excluded that in some cases this danger is connected not so much with the new political thinking, but with the incorrect understanding of its dialectics. In particular, it is not understood that in the problems of this new Philosophy of survival, not What is it, but a historical role was played by the modern defense capabilities of socialism, and that the new political thinking does not exclude, but includes in itself the preservation of military strategic parity.

Not only the class approach, but also the priority of the universal human principle in the modern policy of saving civilization and require that the material forces of militarism and super-murder be opposed by powerful ones for the life and future of the planet. So from me a. For realism, the care for the defense of socialism remains the primary task of the countries and armies of the Warsaw Pact. The fundamental importance of the philosophical and methodological problems of military affairs is also preserved. However, in this area too, the powerful influence of the revolutionary ideas of perestroika and new political thinking is felt.

Philosophy performs methodological functions in the form of extremely general requirements, manifesting themselves as fundamental principles of human cognitive and practical activity.

In its role as methodology, philosophy is a method by which a person reconciles the limited way of his concrete historical and professional existence with the universal dimensions and laws of objective reality. In other words, it is a method of his worldview, or his worldview, but in the form of a method, which is one and the same. This is the indissoluble unity of worldview and methodology. Unfortunately, this unity and especially its influence on the content of the concept of methodology are not always taken into account.

Many philosophical schools and teachings that emerged in the historical development and confrontation of the two main philosophical trends, materialism and idealism, have conveyed certain requirements to war and military affairs. Modern bourgeois philosophy is the unconditional methodological and worldview basis of bourgeois military theory and practice. Although unscientific, it meets the interests of imperialism and actively serves its military intentions and goals in a worldview and methodological sense. From this circumstance arises the task of systematically exposing the reactionary role that modern forms of idealism and metaphysics play in the aggressive policy of imperialism.

The main thing, however, is something else: to reveal the methodological and worldview role of Marxist-Leninist philosophy both in relation to the global problems of military affairs, affecting the interests of all mankind, and in a certain sense also of world history, and in relation to those of its issues that relate to the military defense of socialism. Recently, especially in the conditions of revolutionary renewal processes in the development of socialism, the issue of overcoming conservatism, dogmas, stereotypes, subjectivism in the methodological and worldview culture of the cadres of socialism, including military cadres, has also acquired paramount importance.

Of fundamental importance in this regard is the requirement for a radical break with traditional notions of war and peace and for a qualitatively new approach to the dialectics of war and politics, to the relationship between class and universal human analysis of contemporary history, to military doctrine and the dialectics of International and National Security.

For the final overcoming of stereotypes and schemes of the past, knowledge and adherence to the principles of philosophical materialism, dialectics, and historical materialism play a paramount role.

Perhaps the most important of them is the principle of objectivity, which theoretically derives from the doctrine of Matter as an objective reality, existing outside and independently of human consciousness, and which in practical terms most accurately expresses the immediate needs of real life and social practice.

2.2. OBJECTIVITY ABOVE ALL – AN IMPERATIVE OF THE MODERN APPROACH TO MILITARY AFFAIRS.

It is accepted that, structurally, Marxist-Leninist philosophy is divided into two parts: dialectical materialism and historical materialism. In accordance with this division, methodological requirements can also be divided, albeit conditionally, into two groups: requirements arising from the theoretical positions of materialism, dialectics and epistemology, and requirements arising from the Marxist-Leninist Philosophy of History, which is historical materialism.

Of course, this division is relative. Their indissoluble unity is well known, in which the Philosophy of History arises as a result of the historical union of materialism with dialectics and the successful application of this qualitatively new theoretical philosophical alloy to the philosophical problems of social development.

This is a particularly striking example of the enormous methodological power that arises from the union of materialism with dialectics and which has been applied to human history. It is at the same time an example of the great proximity between the methodological and heuristic functions of philosophical knowledge.

Of the requirements of directive materialism, the most essential for socialist military science and practice is the principle of the objective approach. The theoretical basis of this principle is the dialectical-materialist solution to the fundamental philosophical question. However, it should not be forgotten that Vladimir Ilyich Lenin considered objectivity as an element of dialectics.

Despite their enormous diversity, the phenomena of wars and armed struggle are divided into two large groups: material and spiritual.

Some exist only in the human consciousness. They are the property of the subject, his internal possession, and they influence wars and armed struggle through the changes they cause in the subject's behavior and actions.

Other material phenomena exist outside and independently of the subject and his consciousness. Their influence on combat actions manifests itself along the lines of their inherent mechanical, physical, chemical, biological, technical and other properties and laws.

Historical experience shows that the achievement of military goals has always depended on both the material and spiritual factors of armed struggle.

It is particularly interesting to note that in the light of individual battles, engagements and wars it is difficult to assess which factors played a more powerful role, the material or the spiritual? If somewhere the outcome depended on a clear material inequality between the forces of the warring parties, there are also cases when the final victory was won with smaller material forces and means, but with clear subjective intellectual, organizational, volitional and other advantages of the Army and especially of its command staff.

The Spiritual Forces of the personnel are also actually involved in the preparation and conduct of combat operations. This implies knowing the essence of the human psyche, its sources, the reasons that cause changes in it, the factors that make it powerful or invalidate, its relationship with the material forces and means of combat operations, its influence on the course and outcome of the armed struggle. Now, when armament and combat equipment have acquired exceptional power, these questions have become even more relevant. Does the Soldier remain as great with his desires, aspirations, patriotic feelings, self-denial, ready for heroic feats and immortal deeds, as in the near and distant just wars, or do the material factors of saber wars completely devalue the Spiritual Forces of people, turn them into dead cogs of a colossal Military Machine?

The question of the relationship between the material and the spiritual, the subjective, in wars and armed struggle has other aspects that reveal with even greater force the methodological and worldview significance of the categories of matter and consciousness for military science and practice.

War is one of the most acute forms of social antagonism. In its flames, over 4 billion people have perished and incalculable material and spiritual values have been destroyed. People do not need special training to understand what a terrible scourge War is for them.

But without special, and at the same time philosophical, training, one cannot answer the question: from what causes wars arise - from some evil spirit inherent in Gods and men, or from certain material conditions of people's life, the eternal "bestial nature of man", about which modern bourgeois ideologists so often speak, or from the bestial material interests of a wretched individual, the private owner of the means of production, which is the eternal fate of the human race or a historically transient phenomenon, associated only with socio-economic formations based on private ownership of the means of production.

These questions have a contemporary historical revision. On the one hand, there are the material forces of the danger of a missile-nuclear guillotine, of all humanity, on the other, the contemporary state of reason, which in capitalist countries is also highly militarized, but the peoples do not accept it unconditionally, although they can also fall under its influence. Not to mention socialist countries, where propaganda in favor of wars is prohibited by law.

In the realm of form, these questions can be posed in the following way: are the causes of wars spiritual or material? Obviously, a scientific solution to the question of the emergence and historical fate of war cannot be given without the Marxist-Leninist philosophical doctrine of the essence and relationship of Matter and consciousness, or, more precisely, without the methodological role of this doctrine, without the opportunities it provides for the scientific study of any specific social or other problem in which material and spiritual phenomena are dialectically opposed.

At the same time, it should not be forgotten that ideological speculations about the causes of wars in modern conditions have not diminished. On the contrary, the conduct of local wars and especially the preparation of a global missile-nuclear war is accompanied by a colossal militarization of consciousness in its scale, in which the activity of unscientific idealistic, metaphysical, biological, religious, Malthusian and other ideas and theories does not diminish.

Mikhail Gorbachev emphasizes that: "The militarization of thinking weakens, even completely eliminates, moral restraints on the path to nuclear suicide." (See: Mikhail Gorbachev. With the Leninist Audacity of October. Page 6).

When it comes to the complex interweaving of the material and spiritual forces of modern society in the military sphere, it would be very dangerous not to take into account the way in which the most ugly monster of the 20th century, militarism, subjugates the consciousness of the people of capitalist countries, convincing them that the path to the abyss was the most important. And here, especially important and determining is the monetary dependence in which nuclear weapons have largely shaped the face of the time and in the minds of many, they have become a kind of idol that demands ever new victims.

The problem of the relationship between the material and the spiritual plays an important methodological role in the study and practical application of the principles of military art.

The existence of numerous, mutually contradictory material and spiritual phenomena has rightly confronted military thought with the question: Is there any order in the material processes of armed struggle? Are there any stable connections that commanders and military leaders could rely on in their humane management activities, or must this order be introduced by the military leader with his reason, will, and other subjective qualities. In any case, the principles of military art were spontaneously developed, but the great dispute, whether they are objective or subjective, remained unresolved until the emergence of dialectical materialism.

On the other hand, not only in the past, but also in modern conditions, the violation of objective laws and principles is a widespread phenomenon. Even socialism, which in a qualitatively new way combines historical necessity with the conscious activity of people, has paid a very high price for the voluntaristic trampling of the objective approach.

It turned out in practice that the enormous methodological possibilities of the revolutionary teaching of Marxism-Leninism regarding the essence and role of principles were not used as they should be in the theory and practice of the real construction of socialist society. Many principles remained undisclosed, and others were simply hushed up or grossly trampled on. Due to the critical nature of the times in which we live, it is not excluded that a similar situation will be created in the theory and practice of military art, and in this neuralgic area of the modern world, old and new forms of subjectivist and dogmatic attitude to principles will appear, that is, deviations from the requirements of the objective approach will be allowed.

Here is one of the most essential philosophical and methodological positions of the dead on this issue, as if specially written by Friedrich Engels for contemporary needs. "Principles are not the starting point of research, of its final result... Neither nature nor humanity conforms to principles, but on the contrary, principles are true only to the extent that they correspond to nature and history."

Applied to the objective state of armaments, combat equipment and human material at the end of the 20th century and to the colossal influence of military affairs on the overall politics of the modern world, this statement by Engels means that military art and military science are also on the threshold of a qualitative renewal of their doctrines, principles and concepts.

An example of a bold revolutionary attitude to these issues is the new military doctrine of the Warsaw Pact countries, which outlines not only the political foundations of the military policy of socialism, but also provides some new starting points for the development and reorganization of socialist Military Science and Practice, such as military-strategic Parity at an ever lower level. Equal security for all peoples. Refusal to conduct offensive combat operations and their material, technical and military preparation. Strict mutual control over the state of the armed forces of the opposing blocs. Prohibition of nuclear weapons and their testing. Dissolution of military blocs, elimination of military bases on foreign territories, and so on.

It is obvious that the comprehensive development of these issues and their implementation in practice is a complex problem, depending to a great extent on the way in which the military-political circles of NATO will treat it. Because the political foundations of the doctrine are embedded in the ideas of new political thinking, which express the interests not only of socialism, but also of the entire modern world. This is a doctrine of disarmament to such a threshold that it would provide sufficient means of defense, but would eliminate the sinister possibilities of militarism for universal destruction.

The objective approach to these new problems for military affairs is absolutely necessary, and it must be applied with the same revolutionary consistency and determination with which the path is given to truth, publicity and renewal in all other areas of life. But the connection of military doctrine with the military defense of socialism also remains unconditional. This is clearly stated in the document itself, where it is written that the Warsaw Pact countries consider the highest duty to their peoples to reliably ensure their safety. And this does not threaten anyone, because all peoples have the right to such safety. The question is different: to find and apply in modern military science, as a whole, both from the East and from the West, that measure of national safety and security, of all modern states, countries and peoples, which would have some real value.

Because in the very concept of security, if it is based on the traditional idea of a continuous increase in military power and military supremacy as guarantors of security, a deep contradiction has emerged, which has turned the arms race from a way to strengthen security into a major factor in its destabilization, and in certain circumstances, complete destruction. Failure to understand this fundamentally new truth will lead the world to a state when not only ecology, but also military insecurity will "grab the throat" of the entire world and will no longer let it go until it destroys it. It is the dialectic of security, national, of social systems, of small and large nations, on earth or in space, that reveals to us in the most vivid way the path by which humanity must overcome the demonic evil of militarism. Back in the 19th century, Friedrich Engels wrote that:

"Militarism dominates Europe and devours it. But this militarism hides within itself the seeds of its own destruction . "

(see: Karl Marx, Friedrich Engels, ed. Vol. 20, page 173.)

And further:

"Militarism, like any other historical phenomenon, will perish from the consequences of its own development."

(see: Marx Engels.. Volume 20, p. 173)

What would Engels say today if he had the opportunity to see how not only Europe, but the entire world is in the clutches of militarism, how precisely in its contemporary self-development one of the most powerful objective tendencies of history is emerging and strengthening, to put an end to this sinister force in order to avoid the End of History?

In general, the specific forms of interaction between the material forces and means of war and the spiritual qualities of the fighting people are very diverse. But whatever these forms may be, socialist military science considers them on the basis of the fundamental dialectical-materialist position of the primacy of the material over the spiritual. It is from this absolute in its power of action dependence that the principle of objectivity in the study of military phenomena arises. "objectivity of consideration, not examples and not digressions, but something in itself." This is how Vladimir Ilyich Lenin formulated this dialectical-materialist principle. (See: Lenin. Works. Volume 38. Page 213.)

Furthermore, Renin explicitly emphasizes that: "objective conditions are stronger than good wishes... And that "there is no more dangerous mistake" than mixing and replacing objective requirements with subjective wishes.

And vice versa: one of the deepest sources of the strength and vitality of party politics is its ability to rely on objective processes and trends in the life of the people.

A particularly important place in the content of the objective approach is occupied by the recognition of objective laws and the conscious effort to conceal their essence and comply with the requirements arising from it.

Unfortunately, however, in the conditions and development of the so-called "administrative model" of socialism, this power is not used as it should be. One of the main features and at the same time the cause of its deformations and negative phenomena turned out to be the bureaucratic attitude to a whole series of economic, political, legal and other objective laws. Bureaucracy in this case is one of the dangerous manifestations of subjectivism and arbitrariness in relation to the objective approach, from which it logically follows that the consistent struggle to overcome it is a primary feature and task of restructuring.

The denial of the objective laws of war and armed struggle inevitably confronts the subject of armed struggle with the penultimate alternative: either to accept that he is a helpless toy in the hands of the absolute Chaos dominating the fighting activity, or to go to the opposite point of view that order brings consciousness into this chaos. In both cases, the objective approach loses all meaning.

Throughout its historical development, military thought has also fallen victim to the subjectivist view that war and armed struggle are not subject to any laws.

Very often this was reinforced by the peculiar external nature of the fighting. Even such a great military theorist as Clausewitz placed military talent and genius above the laws.

Clausewitz wrote that: "war is a realm of chance..., and, Three-quarters of what the actions of war are built on, lies in the fog of the unknown." (see: Sankin, V.E. Basic principles of operational art and tactics. Moscow., 1973. Page 30.)

Having adopted this negative attitude towards the objective laws of war and armed struggle, Clausewitz was logically forced to assert that: "talent and genius act independently of laws." (See: Sankin, V.E. Basic principles of operational art and tactics. Moscow, 1973. Page 31.)

The denial of the objective laws of war and armed struggle and the principles of military art arising from them is also characteristic of contemporary representatives of bourgeois Military Thought. An example in this regard in recent years was the American professor Prede, who considered the principles of military art as a "manifestation of human reason" and a product of the creative genius of generals.

For socialist military science, the objective approach is inseparable from the recognition of the objective laws and regularities of wars and armed struggle.

This methodological position gives a strict focus to military research activities towards the study of the objective laws, causes and trends in modern wars, towards the precise formulation of the principles of military art, on the basis of which the management of modern combat operations is carried out, and in accordance with which the peacetime training and education of troops is carried out.

These principles, although they do not exist in the material processes of armed struggle, are the main form through which objective laws make their demands on the subject and occupy a central place in his cognitive and practical Methods.

Such is the deep meaning of Friedrich Engels' popular thought regarding the nature of human domination over nature: "at every step we are reminded that we do not dominate nature at all in the same way as a conqueror of a foreign people dominates, as someone who stands outside of nature... Our entire domination over it consists in the fact that we have the advantage over all other creatures of knowing and correctly applying its laws." (see: Marx, Engels. Works. Volume 20. Page 485.) However, I would like to emphasize once again that the objective approach of military cadres can be mastered only if it is combined with the methodological possibilities of another approach - the concrete one.

Objectivity contains within itself concreteness. Deprived of the direct connection with the object under study, objectivity can become an empty sound.

Applied specifically to modern warfare, to the material forces that humanity keeps in constant and full combat readiness and can call into action at any moment, objectivity demands a profound reassessment of traditional views on war. This is precisely what characterizes the military aspects of the new political thinking, which offers the whole world the advantages of a realistic approach over the schemes, illusions, and delusions of the recent past.

- the objective state of military phenomena at the modern stage poses great challenges to military science. It is also on the threshold of profound revolutionary changes that will inevitably affect all areas of military affairs, from its material foundations in the form of military production, armaments and military equipment, to military doctrines, the principles of military art and the strategy and tactics of their application in the organization and conduct of combat operations. Qualitative changes are also inevitable in the construction and personnel policy of the armed forces, as well as in the organization and nature of peacetime training of troops. But in order to avoid any manifestations of subjectivism of a new type, it is necessary that these transformations imposed by the time in which we live be carried out under the sign of increased quality in the care of the defense of socialism.

When he touches on the objective changes that have occurred and are occurring in contemporary international relations and, above all, the new historical possibilities of power politics, Mikhail Gorbachev emphasizes that it is precisely these changes that "determine our defense construction, the effectiveness of which in the future should be ensured primarily by qualitative parameters - both in terms of technology and military science, and in terms of the composition of the armed forces." (see: materials of the 19th All-Union Conference. Moscow 1988. Page 83.).

2.3. WARS BEFORE THE COURT OF REASON AND THE CULTURE OF NATIONS. THE NEW POLITICAL THINKING - A MANIFESTO FOR SAVING HUMANITY FROM DESTRUCTION.

The objective approach is a necessary but insufficient methodological beginning in the study of military phenomena. Left to itself, detached from people's consciousness, it easily degenerates into objectivism, into a kind of reverse subjectivism.

Of essential importance for the scientific approach to military phenomena at the contemporary stage are also the methodological requirements arising from the dialectical-materialist doctrine of the essence of consciousness and its role in the historical process.

However, proceeding to the disclosure of the essence and role of human consciousness, we are obliged to do this as materialists. It is especially important not to forget that it is here, on the "territory" of ideas, in the kingdom of the "spirit", in the emotional and volitional manifestations of people, that numerous dangers arise for violation of the methodological requirements of materialism, for various manifestations of subjective arbitrariness in relation to objective circumstances. And the greater the role of ideas in one or another objectively arising historical process, such as the modern era, modern war, the construction of modern socialism, and others, - the stricter the requirement for an objective approach.

However, this requirement should in no case be treated as an attempt or tendency to underestimate the role of consciousness in cognitive and practical activity. Dialectical, and precisely dialectical materialism, is characterized by the recognition of the creative role of ideas, consciousness, thinking, Spiritual phenomena, in social development. Moreover, dialectical materialism affirms the extremely important methodological point of view that the natural historical process cannot be realized if it is not supported by the action of the corresponding, adequate consciousness. In methodological terms, this dependence requires that the principle of the objective approach be combined in the most decisive way with another principle - about the active and creative attitude of human consciousness to the objective natural and social processes taking place outside and independently of it.

This requirement has been repeatedly emphasized by the classics of Marxism-Leninism. We will recall some of them: ""Ideas become material force, as soon as they seize the masses" (see: Karl Marx. Works. Volume One. Page 402.), "consciousness not only reflects the world, but also creates..." (see: Vladimir Ilyich Lenin. Works. Volume 38. Page 204).

The following thought of Vladimir Ilyich Lenin is particularly characteristic: "Marxism is distinguished from all other social theories by the remarkable combination of complete scientific sobriety, in the analysis of the objective state of things, and the objective course of evolution, with the most resolute recognition of the importance of revolutionary energy, revolutionary creativity, and the revolutionary initiative of the masses..."

It should be emphasized right away that it is precisely in this combination of the objective approach with the high revolutionary activity of the working people that the intransigence, vitality and strength of socialist society lies. But only in those cases when this combination is not deformed in the direction of formal verbal declarations, as is the case with the bureaucratic model of socialism. Such deformations can be especially dangerous for the development of socialism, and can have catastrophic consequences and results.

In short, materialism in unity with dialectics, that is, dialectical materialism, is equally alien to both objectivism, caudateism and fatalism, which deny the active and creative role of ideas in history, and to subjectivism, which exaggerates this role and denies their dependence and secondaryness on the material conditions and the objective laws of the historical process. Objectivity - yes, but not objectivism. Subjectivity - yes, but not subjectivism. Objectivity and subjectivity in an indissoluble unity, in which the first is determining, and the second is secondary and derivative, but a necessary prerequisite and condition for the realization of philosophical materialism. In modern conditions, these fundamental philosophical and methodological dependencies have received a new concretization, corresponding to the new historical realities.

Now the subjective side of the historical process is embedded in the requirements for revolutionary thinking, for a radical breakthrough in science, art, culture, and education, for a multifaceted, and in perspective, comprehensive development of the personality, uniting within itself both modern, responding to the scientific and technical revolution, intellectual and professional training with an unwavering scientific worldview and high general culture.

From a methodological point of view. Any process, including the reconstruction of socialism, can develop successfully only if it is combined with adequate awareness of the people.

And since the restructuring itself is a revolutionary process, the changes in consciousness also require revolutionary changes. Without these changes, the construction of a new life is impossible.

This is a fundamental principle of party policy in the spiritual sphere, which is fully, without any restrictions, also valid for the formation of consciousness in the socialist armies. And this is not only because the personnel are an inseparable part of the people, but because the objective state of military problems to no less extent requires New Revolutionary Thinking, a qualitatively new level of intellectual, worldview and military professional training of the entire personnel . So the restructuring is also "knocking" on the doors of the armed forces. In philosophical and methodological terms, the state and role of Spiritual factors in military affairs cannot be limited only to what is typical of socialist armies.

Now a historical dialogue is being conducted between the reason of life and the madness of war. We have already drawn attention to the fact that in the capitalist world and especially in the armies of imperialism an unprecedented militarization of the Spiritual Forces of the people is taking place. In this completely irresponsible and dangerous for the peoples activity the entire ideological front of the bourgeoisie takes an active part - philosophers and politicians, clergymen and scientists, a large part of the artistic intelligentsia. The technical possibilities of the militaristic debauchery of the Spiritual Forces - cinema, radio, television, school, church for the press and literature, are enormous. Not to mention the bourgeois armies, where everything is recognized in this chariot of death. With the help of old concepts, new and new ones are being developed to impress upon modern man that war should be preferred to Peace, that armament is a guarantor of security, that the modern James Bond, this is the notorious Rambo, who has dedicated himself to the fight against the Reds. It is no longer enough to say that this is something like playing with fire, because the subordination of the Spiritual Forces of people to war, the cult of nuclear War and its cosmic and stellar variants, are a super crime that destroys the natural immune systems of human consciousness and cultivates in it blind aggressiveness.

It is hardly necessary to prove that the ideological process of the armed forces of socialism, the main goal and task of which is to form the fighting spirit of the personnel, cannot be abstracted from, not taking into account the unceasing ideological and psychological activity of militarism.

Of course, these questions concerning the connection of the Spiritual Forces of the peoples with the problems of war and peace and of military affairs as a real, National stubborn National force of modernity, can far from be attributed to the ideological exploits and crime of militarism. The picture of the spiritual attitude to war today is much more complex. The process of forming this picture is also more complex. Although slowly, in this process the influence of the main objective trend of modern history is increasingly felt - the unity of peoples in the struggle for the survival of the human race. Scientists understand this best now. Instinctively, a part of the professional heralds of the military lovers are approaching the same understanding along this path.

It seems that the last refuge in the spiritual plague of militarism will be the armies of the old society. And this is logical. Whatever vicissitudes this process goes through, Whatever difficulties it encounters, its main tendency leads and will crystallize in the so-called planetary consciousness, in which the image of the enemy, taking on the characteristics of nations and people, must be and will be replaced by the image of a unified humanity, which, despite its enormous diversity, including the existence of different social systems, is based on trust, equality, freedom of social choice, cooperation and other such factors.

And if someone thinks that these are illusions born of a complete break with the requirements of a class approach to the prospects of social consciousness and its core ideology, such a revolutionary can be answered in only one way: If the Spiritual Forces are fatally doomed to class confrontation, if this confrontation is always maintained in the same tense, to the extreme, ideological state, if this tension is constantly growing, and then when not only in the mind, but also before the eyes of humanity, the terrible dimensions of universal nuclear destruction are outlined, then no other future can be predicted for such humanity than what the Philosophy of Fatalism foretells for it.

As for the class approach, it remains in force, but in order to avoid its vulgarization, it should be taken into account that history is entering a special era when, "without losing their class character, international relations are increasingly being realized as relations between peoples." (see: Mikhail Gorbachev. With Lenin's Wisdom and Responsibility. Page 560).

It seems that the dialectical contradiction between the voice and the universal is a real riddle for dogmatism. In its schemes, the class approach is transformed from a means of revolutionary struggle of the working class into some kind of self-serving fetish and idol. It is not understood the simplicity and at the same time the great truth that the ideal of revolutionary Maxim and low theory is a united humanity, without classes, class struggle, without exploitation, without oppression and without violence. Now, however, a little expected, but with enormous power of action, tendency is emerging, for humanity to unite before the victory of communism in the sphere of material conditions. To unite not on a communist basis as This was reflected in communist ideals, long before that, and on a Democratic basis, connected with the historical necessity to save civilization from the mortal dangers that have arisen in the bowels of society, in social existence, among which militarism occupies the first place.

But in all likelihood, this will be a very long and difficult process, in which fierce resistance to militarism may make the hope of survival even more fragile.

That is why ideological vigilance against the apology of war will be preserved, and as the main law of the development of the Spiritual Forces of the whole society. And, of course, the main force of the struggle against the ideology of militarism will be the class Marxist-Leninist doctrine of peace, war and the army. It is precisely the class doctrine, and there is and cannot be any doubt about this.

But this doctrine has also faced the tests of time, the need for profound renewal. Perhaps it is to it that the requirement to break with some of the ossified dogmas and stereotypes of thought from that Philosophy of War, which reflected the military phenomena of the Tomato period, but in the new conditions no longer corresponds to history, applies most strongly.

Sometimes the inconvenience of admitting this is associated with one or another of the classics' statements. There are even more serious cases when one's own theoretical helplessness and tendency to dogmatism are hidden behind the classics' statements, as the subject of special speculation are those of their positions that relate primarily to the class nature of military phenomena. But this has already been discussed elsewhere in this presentation. Here we will only note that from a methodological point of view, when revealing the projection of nuclear war in the spiritual sphere of the modern world, it is necessary to be guided by the following basic position: the most important modern manifestation of historical necessity is not that this or that person be defeated, not that this or that system be removed from the historical scene, not that this or that people be directed to some almost obligatory direction of social development, not that this or that class be given historical priority. In general, not what divides the world into opposites and Which is also written in the contemporary manifestation of historical necessity. And this is written with an impressive force unknown in history.

This state of affairs is the result of the contradictions between the opposites, which were just mentioned. But precisely because of this state of contradictions, and especially because of the enormous social forces involved in the conflict between them, that tendency and side of historical necessity has come to the fore in the action of historical necessity which demands that humanity survive. And this is not some wish that can be argued about. This is the truth above all truths, an absolute truth, an axiom, a tendency without an alternative.

What historical courage and strength do the words of Mikhail Gorbachev radiate in this regard: "we have made our choice... To ignore what divides us for the sake of common human interests, for the sake of life on earth." (see: Mikhail Gorbachev. Perestroika and New Thinking..., page 172.).

And if, nevertheless, someone from the left or the right, from either side of the confrontation between the two main trends of modern World History that have thus emerged, the trend of polarization and contradictions leading to the Abyss of Non-Existence, and the trend of unity of the modern world, expressed in the highest value of this earth called humanity, continues to rely on what divides the world, then such a person must be classified as a "troglodyte" regardless of the labels he puts on his ideas. Because, as Karl Marx emphasizes, "the label of a system of views differs from the labels of other givens in that it often deceives not only the buyer, but also the seller." (see: Karl Marx, Friedrich Engels. Works. Volume 24. Page 405.).

And on the occasion of this mass warning against the possibilities of self-deception, we will note a few things: first, Isn't it time to seriously think about the consequences of the monopoly on truth that some "Marxists" persistently impose in the fight against non-Marxist views? Second, Isn't it time to understand that even in the fight of ideas it is unacceptable to divide things into two colors: Marxism and Anti-Marxism? A very strong, but not always strong tendency in the sphere of ideas, that the polarization of Spiritual Forces between truth and error is a far more complex process than, for example, separating them in a flock into white sheep from black ones. And now, on the issues of war and peace, this process has taken a hundred times more complex form, because life, survival are preferred to universal destruction not only by Marxists and not only by the positions of this truly Great Teaching called Marxism-Leninism? Thirdly, isn't it more logical to assume that in the spiritual sphere, in the various levels and forms of public consciousness, a process of rapprochement of the universal, the democratic with the class will begin, and more precisely has already begun, and this rapprochement may prove to be especially necessary for ideologies where such a front is vocally elevated to a cult, and the fact that survival as a fundamental interest of humanity is more vital and deeper than class interests, which also cause the ideological polarization of the Spiritual Forces of the peoples, is not taken into account. Why, for example, not to raise the question of ideological cooperation within the framework of those issues that have a universal human character. What will humanity lose from such cooperation and what will it gain if the dominant tendency of ideological opposition tends towards the notorious "image of the enemy". It is time for these questions to be addressed to the positions of ideological dogmatism, because its revolutionary phraseology makes it more covert, but not safer for the revolutionary struggle of the communist movement. In general, the question of dogmatism and the heavy damage that it inflicted on socialist construction should be referred to Slavov's developed questions of the theory of the construction of today's class society. Bets on dogmatism, which functioned as the ideology of the bureaucratic period of the development of socialism. For tomatoes, which turned into a restored argument of its infallibility, and in essence on the issues of war and peace did not give Who knows what contribution to stopping, or at least slowing down the sinister process of moving towards the danger of universal destruction.

These are new trends in the development of the spiritual life and the Spiritual Forces of modern society, reflecting the corresponding laws of the special historical era into which it enters world history. Precisely a historical era! It seems that the period of growing confrontation between capitalism and socialism has reached such a Critical point beyond which there is no prospect for anyone. Socialism has managed to achieve Parity on many issues and has thus created material prerequisites for being Recognized as an equal partner now and in further development. The hopes of the worst enemies of socialism to turn history back using military means have been convincingly refuted.

But even dogmatism (in socialism) must reconsider some of its views:

For example, the hope that the demise of capitalism is a matter of the foreseeable historical future, or that capitalism has exhausted all its possibilities for the development of productive forces, or a view of the absolute unsuitability of the economic system of capitalism and the impossibility of its being reformed in a democratic direction, or the possibilities of bourgeois democracy developing in some countries in a very wide range of democracy, which creates great, still poorly studied and poorly used peaceful possibilities for the progress of humanity.

In general, integration trends in the development of the consciousness of peoples are now gaining paramount importance, as a response and reflection of the relevant parties in the action of historical necessity and the objective laws of modern overall social development. In the light of these trends, the forecasts made by the 19th Congress of the Communist Party of the Soviet Union regarding the most likely near future of humanity are understandable, namely:

-demilitarization and humanization of international relations.

- dominance of reason and knowledge over selfish aspirations and prejudices in resolving the numerous contradictions in the world.

- balance of interests and the right to free choice for development.

- wise use of the international power of scientific and technical potential to solve global problems: ecological, economic, energy, medical, food, educational, demographic and other such problems.

- security based on political interaction instead of security based on military potentials.

- mutual enrichment of national and regional cultures based on voluntary communication and trust between peoples, regardless of the social choices they have made for their development.

And all this must be done and accomplished not in the name of mutual outsmarting, but only for the sake of peace, which has become a symbol of life.

Here is a very characteristic statement in this regard: "rising above the limited understanding of class and national interests, above ideological and other differences. The two world social systems are rivals in the struggle of ideas, but they must be partners in the struggle to preserve life on earth." And further, even more clearly: "" in the Nuclear Age... It is necessary to think and act in planetary dimensions, to put common human interests at the forefront, to master the difficult art of living with each other, not against each other."

However, we should not turn the forecast made into a source of ideological blindness to contemporary realities, because the imperialist roots of aggression and war have not disappeared, militarism continues to threaten the world, and guarantees for the irreversibility of the positive processes that have begun have not yet been created. This also determines the defense policy of socialism.

The dialectical approach to this issue obliges us to emphasize that militarism will continue to poison the spiritual atmosphere of international relations.

In addition to new trends, it is likely that for a long time we will hear not the Echo, but the direct manifestations of militarism in philosophy and ethics, in political doctrines and religion, in the artistic sphere, and in natural science.

In the program of the CPSU, adopted at the 27th Congress, it is unnecessarily and correctly emphasized that "the arms monopolies, the generals, the state bureaucracy, the ideological apparatus and militarized science, which have merged into the military-industrial complex, have become the most zealous conductors and organizers of the policy of adventurism and aggression."

And this complex, also called "the most difficult and terrible monster of the twentieth century", and "the iceberg of death", will continue to desperately seek "profit at any cost, even if the very building in which the bourgeoisie lives, vibrates from the accelerating revolutions of the arms race." (see: Volkogonov. Psychological warfare. Page 239.)

The following data speak eloquently about the current revolutions of this flywheel: 164 companies in the United States of America receive from the military industry from 50% to 200% profit, three of them receive over 500% profit, one of them over 2000 percent profit. How can one not fulfill on this occasion that thought of Karl Marx, where he compares capital to a pagan idol that does not want to drink nectar in any other way than from the skulls of murdered people. And to a vampire that, at 300% profit, is ready to commit any crime, even in those cases when the noose of the gallows hangs over his head. Here, with the ideologists of this monster, a struggle will be waged for a long time, including a philosophical and methodological one, over the causes of wars, past and present, and the role of ideas, feelings, desires, will in their incitement. Struggle over the influence of Spiritual factors in the preparation and conduct of wars and armed struggle. Struggle over the interaction of material forces and the objective laws of wars with the so-called fighting spirit of the warring peoples and armies. Struggle over the diametrical opposition of the ideas with which the different armies are armed. Struggle over the methods and criteria for forming the spiritual and moral-political potential of a given army. And all this, of course, is subordinated to certain goals.

In the conditions of military ideological confrontation, the listed issues are not resolved in the same way under socialism and capitalism. On the contrary, there is a diametrically opposed approach to them, or in other words, if under socialism the theoretical methodological basis for considering these problems is the Marseille-Leninist philosophical doctrine of consciousness, in capitalist armies the role of the theoretical basis is primarily played by idealistic concepts of consciousness.

What, more specifically, are the starting methodological solutions to the above questions in the Marxist-Leninist and bourgeois approaches to them?

First, Marxism-Leninism rejects the view that the causes of wars lie somewhere in the spiritual sphere. There are not a small number of idealist philosophers who seek the roots of war horrors in consciousness. Some view wars as punishment for the human race imposed by the spirit of God. Others proceed from the indefinable aggressive nature of the human spirit. Still others absolutize the biological in man in order to explain wars with all sorts of human instincts. Still others speculate on the aggressive spiritual qualities of kings, monks, prominent military and political figures.

These views are an expression of the desire to hide from the eyes and minds of the people the true causes of the war. From a methodological point of view.

According to the Marxist-Leninist philosophical doctrine of consciousness in the spiritual sphere of humanity there are and cannot be any reasons for wars. Consciousness is a reflection of being in. And if aggressive ideas appear in consciousness, this is a signal that in the sphere of material conditions there are reasons from which these ideas arise. And it is these reasons that lead not only to militaristic ideologies, but also to real wars. A typical example in this regard is modern capitalism. The cult of war and violence, characteristic of modern bourgeois ideology, is not the work of either heaven or the criminal, earthly spirit. In this cult is expressed the indelible aggressive nature of the exploitation of man by man. Millionaires in the past and billionaires now strive for wars with the same force with which working people reject them. The former, driven by the Insatiable Thirst for profit, the latter because of their meaninglessness and horrors.

As for socialism, it destroys the roots of war in the material sphere and on this basis adopts the idea of eternal peace in

relations between peoples. In this connection, the bourgeois thesis about Red militarism, about the aggressive nature of communist ideas, about the Soviet danger should be attributed to the category of the most monstrous lies that have ever arisen in the sphere of consciousness. Red militarism does not and cannot exist. But, the military power of socialism, capable of deterring lovers of military adventures, exists and will exist, As long as this is necessary.

This is one of the main laws of socialist construction, arising from the way world history began and developed after the Great October Socialist Revolution.

Secondly, the Marxist-Leninist philosophical doctrine of consciousness is the only methodology on the basis of which a correct answer to the question can be found:

Why do some classes adopt some military ideologies, while others adopt radically opposite ones? And one more thing: Why do some military ideologies take over hatred of people, and moralism, banditry, racism, chauvinism and other such things? Why is it necessary for millions of people, who have fallen under the influence of such brutal ideologies, to lose their human image, to turn into "a strange breed of wild beasts", professional killers, freed even from the restraints of conscience, capable of any crimes? Because no class can freely choose its ideas. Consciousness is a reflection of being. What is being, such is consciousness. If capital dominates being, from all the pores of which human sweat and human blood flows, then the reflection of this being can only be one thing - aggressive ideology!

Socialism also cannot choose its military ideology. Just as the bourgeoisie is not able to use Marxism-Leninism, so socialism cannot make the ideas of the bourgeoisie its banner. Socialist ideology, including its military aspects, is highly humane not by the will and desires of this or that person, but by virtue of true humanism, which for the first time in all human history is asserting itself in the sphere of material relations between people.

In short, socialism must be prepared to wage wars against armies that have been subjected to complete ideological debauchery in advance. This is natural. And in these wars socialism cannot have any other banner than humanism, taken in the broadest sense of the word: as a matter of defending the conquests of socialism; as an opportunity in the course of the war to support the efforts for the social and national liberation of other peoples; as a struggle for peace against the forces of war; for compliance with various agreements regarding the ways and means of waging wars themselves, as a comprehensive concern for man.

Thirdly, on the methodological basis of the Marxist-Leninist philosophical doctrine of consciousness, the question of the role of consciousness - ideas, feelings, psyche - in wars is also developed.

The military experience of history presents the role of the spiritual factor in a different light. There are cases when it seems that an army drew strength from this factor. On the other hand, they lost their fighting spirit, their determination to win, to achieve the goals of the war, and thus they owned their defeat. The military experience of socialism has demonstrated a new solution to this question. The spiritual factor, also called the moral-political factor, has become a special kind of weapon that creates gigantic advantages for the socialist army. The military ideologists and practitioners of imperialism watch this weapon with envy and fear, but they are not able to forge it either in factories or in the ideological sphere. But they cannot destroy it either!

Where does this difference in the role of the spiritual factor come from? Why is it in some cases a terrible kind of weapon that makes fighting people stronger than death, and in others its role is the opposite? Why, for example, in the last war against the Vietnamese people, 350 thousand soldiers deserted from the army of the United States of America? After all, this army is carrying out a huge ideological work, the purpose of which is to forge reliable, ideological foundations for combat activity.

The Marxist-Leninist philosophical doctrine of consciousness teaches us that ideas are not a sword that can be thrown onto the battlefield and further serve the enemy. Ideas, This is the form in which the belligerents realize the war, its goals, their place, the meaning or meaninglessness of the blood shed and the horrors experienced. And this awareness is tailored to the measure of the socio-economic Formation and the attitude that it has in the war and towards the belligerents. From here we can now answer the question, Why imperialism cannot use the Spiritual weapons of the socialist Armies and why the fighting spirit of the bourgeois armies is always inferior to that of the socialist armies. Because these are spiritual weapons of two opposing social systems. Because in these weapons are reflected and taken the form of consciousness, both the enormous historical advantages of socialism, for which working people are consciously ready for anything, and the historical doom of capitalism, its anti-human nature, the contradictions between capital and labor, because of which working people can go to battle only if they are deceived or forcibly extorted, or ideologically and spiritually devastated and depraved.

Fourth, the methodological significance of the Marxist-Leninist philosophical doctrine for consciousness, for the correct approach to the methods and criteria of military training and education is enormous. This question has many aspects: analysis of historical experience; the qualitative difference between the methods applied in the socialist and bourgeois armies; the enormous diversity of specific methods of training and education in the socialist army; the problem of the effectiveness and criteria of the methods. The methodological significance is contained in the first aspect - the principled solution to the question of the theoretical basis on which the methods for forming the spiritual potential of a given army are developed.

At first glance, one may get the impression that the choice of methods of education is entirely up to the educators and depends entirely on their talent. Such an impression is wrong. It can become a theoretical premise for an even more wrong idea that in modern bourgeois armies any methods can be used, including those that are used in the formation of the spiritual potential of socialist armies. Or, conversely, that in socialist armies the use of methods used in bourgeois armies is allowed and permissible.

In the choice and practical application of Methods of Education the role of skill and talent is indisputable, and is very large. But this choice moves within strictly defined limits, arising from the essence and content of the goals set. When it comes to the formation of spiritual potential in the modern armies of imperialism. The methods of education are necessarily predetermined by the Spiritual qualities that this education should create in the personnel. It must present socialism in a false light. And this can be achieved by deception, slander and lies. It must also present capitalism in a false light. And this goal logically leads to the methods of deception. If someone does not succumb to deception, coercion comes into force. And for all who succumb to ideological corruption, means are used for the spiritual devastation of the human personality, for the transformation of entire armies into organized gatherings of bandits and murderers, such as the army of fascism.

It is hardly necessary to prove the absolute inapplicability of the indicated methods in the socialist armies. The spiritual potential of the socialist armies reflects in itself the interests of the military defense of socialism. These are to a high degree humane interests and their awareness by the personnel necessarily requires to the same extent humane Methods. The main epistemological advantage of these methods is that they are in unity with the truth. And when it comes to the formation of spiritual potential, the truth is all-powerful both as a goal and as a means. In this way, the objective boundaries within which the Choice of Methods of Education in the socialist armies moves are outlined. These are boundaries excluding any delusions and forms of unconstitutional and illegal coercion. With skillful pedagogical, methodological and other application, these methods are able to provide the personnel of the socialist armies with a qualitatively new type of fighting spirit, the advantages of which were magnificently demonstrated in the war of the Soviet army for the defense of the socialist Fatherland.

Of course, it must be absolutely clear that this fighting spirit will prove powerless before the omnipotent element of nuclear war. But it is absolutely necessary now, when a gigantic struggle is being waged unsymbolically to prevent this flood. That is why the view that the impossibility of a winner in a nuclear war led to the meaninglessness of military labor in the armed forces of socialism is deeply mistaken.

No, simply the meaning of this Work has changed qualitatively - to block the forces of death, because, as Karl Marx taught, "material power can only be overthrown by material power." And can there really be a higher meaning, and a higher historical responsibility, than this? We will emphasize once again: the question of the directions, tasks and goals of ideological work cannot be decided in the spirit of stereotypes from the past. It is best to bring it into line with the state and dialectical development of military affairs at the modern stage.

2.4. FOR A QUALITATIVELY NEW APPROACH TO THE DIALECTICS OF THE DEVELOPMENT OF MILITARY AFFAIRS IN THE MODERN STAGE. THE IMPERATIVE OF THE DEFENSIVE MILITARY DOCTRINE.

In the general system of Marxism-Leninism, dialectics occupies a special place. Vladimir Ilyich Lenin defined it as the revolutionary soul of Marxism. Its laws and categories are a subjective image of objective dialectics. Its revolutionary heuristic methodological power stems from the fact that natural and social processes themselves proceed dialectically. To apply a dialectical approach and method means that the method and approach, as means standing on the side of the subject, should be an analogue, an image, a reflection of the way in which objective reality changes and develops. In a word, this is materialist dialectics.

These preliminary considerations are necessary in order to exclude any attempts to oppose the dialectics of materialism. There is no and cannot be a dialectic "above" objective reality. This situation also contains an important methodological requirement for the military cadres of socialism; the dialectical method as a system of methodological principles and requirements must be studied and applied creatively, in the closest connection and in inseparable unity with the objective dialectics of the real processes in modern military affairs.

The dialectical nature of military phenomena and processes, and the need for a dialectical approach to them, is given great attention in almost all scientific studies of military problems.

Here it is not necessary, nor impossible, to make a comprehensive and detailed analysis of the manifestation of genetic laws and categories in military affairs. We will dwell only on some basic methodological requirements that have acquired particularly great importance in the development of military phenomena in the modern era. First of all, materialist dialectics requires that military affairs be studied in its own development. In general, the idea of development is one of the basic ideas of dialectics.

The consideration of dialectical categories without reference to development obscures both their content and their methodological role. In this sense, dialectics can be defined as a doctrine of development, and this does not at all deprive us of the right to consider it as a doctrine of universal connection, or to raise the question of the "core" of this doctrine, which can also be used as a starting point for a definition.

As a methodological tool of military knowledge, the doctrine of development has a very wide range of manifestations and applications. It is the theoretical basis of the historical approach, with the help of which the truth about the military history of society is revealed. The elimination of wars from the life of nations is an inseparable question of their emergence and development. Without a scientific answer to this question, the possibility, or impossibility, of creating a society without war cannot be substantiated. In modern conditions, this question is of paramount importance in the ideological struggle between socialism and capitalism. In addition, the dialectical idea of studying military affairs in "its own movement", in its own life" remains valid and occupies an important place in the training of the armed forces of socialism and especially its military cadres. (See: Vladimir Ilyich Lenin. Works. Volume 38. Page 214.).

The methodological and heuristic role of the direct idea of

development is revealed through the numerous requirements and principles that arise from the laws and categories of materialist dialectics. For the study of changes in modern warfare, the following requirements have acquired particular importance:

- to reveal the existing opposing sides, properties and trends in the development of war and armed struggle.

- to reveal the contradictions in the struggle between these opposites, with particular attention paid to the basic, internal and main ones, which determine the dominant trends in the development of military affairs and play an important methodological role in military forecasting.

- to reveal and resolve the so-called subjective contradictions, which arise from the incorrect actions of the subjective factor and negatively affect the development of socialist Military Science.

- to reveal the qualitative changes in military affairs. Unlike the past, they are distinguished by a very great depth and speed of progress, which constantly confronts military knowledge and practice with new, extremely complex problems.

- socialist military science should systematically study the growing influence of modern military phenomena on the economy, science, technology, politics, ideology, and all spiritual and natural factors.

A number of methodological requirements arising from the categories of dialectics have also acquired significant importance. For example, it is necessary to take into account the special way of manifestation of the dialectic between necessity and chance, and above all the visibly increased role of chance both in the emergence of modern wars and in the processes of armed struggle.

"The more nuclear weapons there are," Mikhail Gorbachev emphasizes, "the less chance there is of their, so to speak, "obedient behavior."

The spread of this weapon, the complication of the technical means associated with it, the increase in the scale of its transportation, the constant possibility of technical errors, manifestations of human weakness or someone's evil will - all this... Is a huge number of coincidences on which the fate of humanity depends."

These accidents also need control, even in socialist armies, however difficult that may be.

It is necessary to study the specifics of the dialectic between the content of war and armed struggle, and the forms of its manifestation. Rapid changes in the content cause a significantly faster elimination of some forms and the emergence of a need to replace them with new ones. This applies with particular force to the dialectic of modern means of armed struggle and the new forms and methods developed by military science for their combat use.

Of great scientific and practical interest are the requirements arising from the way in which the dialectical interaction in the military field between the categories of "possibility" and "reality" takes place. Perhaps it is these two categories that should become a starting philosophical and methodological point of view. For the formation of a qualitatively new vision of the dialectical state of modern military affairs.

Let us take up the question of contradictions again. Now they have been brought to a state that in many places borders on the absurd. For example, for centuries the contradiction between the goals and the means of armed struggle has resulted in a continuous development of armaments in order to achieve the set goals with greater certainty, and a continuous change in the goals themselves, corresponding to the increased combat capabilities of new weapons. In nuclear weapons this process can be considered completed, and according to the logic of dialectics that comes into effect when opposites are transformed into each other.

Now, unlike in the past, it is pointless to link any goals with the further development of nuclear weapons. In this regard, possibility has been replaced by impossibility, and the transition of military affairs to the plane of defense doctrines has acquired the character of an objective historical necessity.

But it immediately follows that the creation of new, as they call them exotic, weapons is more a result of the inertia of old thinking than of logic, and secondly, for some circles this logic is transferred to the many times larger profits that are obtained from the military business.

Or let's take other contradictions; security-armament, economy-war, morality-war, ecology-war, others can be mentioned.

In each of these respects, warfare has acquired the character of an absurd force. Everything that stands in the way of this force, nature or material production, politics or morality, science or technology, culture or religion, everything from the individual to nations and civilization as a whole, will be ruthlessly destroyed. It is warfare in its nuclear period of development that has given rise to a whole chain of paradoxes, imperatives and absurdities, with which nuclear thinking is powerless to cope and has begun to resemble Stone Age thinking.

An imperative of survival, an ecological imperative, a paradox of absurd politics that is unable to stop the flywheel of the arms race, a moral imperative, a paradox of Rozova, which proves powerless to explain the absurdities of militarism. These are such contradictions that no longer prove, but rather show how that self-denial of militarism, which Friedrich Engels spoke about in the last century, is being carried out in practice.

If things go in a tragic direction, including due to reasons of a random nature, which have already been discussed, there is only one way out of these contradictions, the elimination of militarism before the Fall of Capitalism, and the translation of military affairs onto the basis of a common defense doctrine for all.

This can happen, no matter how unacceptable it may seem, from the point of view of the dogmatic understanding of the class approach to international relations.

And this must happen, and it will happen, because there is no reasonable alternative, because the objective dialectical logic of existence demands it.

2.5. EPISTEMOLOGY AND MILITARY AFFAIRS. THE NUCLEAR IRRATIONALISM OF THE TWENTIETH CENTURY.

Epistemology is a field in the cognitive activity of the subject where all methodological requirements for both theory and practice come together in a unique way. And this is no coincidence.

Karl Marx characterized knowledge as the basic form of consciousness, from which it logically follows that in the paths and methods to knowledge one can expect sharper clashes between different philosophical concepts and a more urgent need for a scientific philosophical methodology.

Moreover, knowledge is a deeply contradictory process that meanders between the sensory and the logical, the abstract and the concrete, the logical and the historical, truth and error, theory and practice, the object and the subject, the objective and the subjective, the material and the ideal, knowledge and ignorance, the relative and the absolute. Taking into account the millennial striving of class egoism, which deliberately gives priority to error and lies, we can explain why Marx compared the path of Science to steep and rocky paths and why I. Dietzgen noticed that in the Philosophy of Knowledge, which is epistemology, almost all representatives of idealism lay their eggs as in a lice pit.

In the cognitive process there is a constant possibility for the mind to incline its efforts towards one, any of the indicated opposites, in order to obtain at the same time a violation of some methodological principle and some manifestation of subjectivism. In modern conditions all this is a hundred times more possible, because the historical peaks to which human knowledge has been brought have significantly increased the tension of the contradictions of its development.

In the military sphere, things are even more complicated both in principle and with the peculiarities of development at the modern stage. Here the clash between the opposites of knowledge is very much like a clash between warring armies. The contradictions are sharp and the struggle of ideas, concepts, doctrines is uncompromising. Let us take as an example one of the classical problems of the theory of knowledge, the problem of the knowability of the world and its philosophical and methodological projection on military phenomena.

As is known, the starting principle of the Marxist-Leninist methodology is the principle of the knowability of the world and its objective laws. It is in the Light and on the basis of this principle that a constant struggle is waged against agnosticism, which in its timid epistemological forms cannot get rid of its doubts about the reliability of knowledge and the principle possibility of achieving it. In its new class manifestations, it loses its timidity and actively, sometimes fiercely, but in all cases deliberately, defends mysticism and irrationalism before the truth. This line in the behavior of agnosticism is very typical and strong for the contemporary state of social science in the turbulent world. (See: Iribadzhakov. N. Philosophy and style of thinking and action. Sofia. 1985. Page 205.). There is a widespread activation of irrationalism, despite the fact that the horizons of the scientific and technical Revolution have qualitatively new historical dimensions. (See: Yankov. M. The Materialistic Dialectics Against Irrationalism. Sofia 1989.).

In this case, one should not underestimate a principled position related to the difference between the knowledge of nature and the knowledge of social phenomena.

The social facts of antagonistic socio-economic formations have clashed with common sense with greater sharpness, and have given rise, first in a vague, and then in a theoretical, scientific form, to the erroneous idea that unknowable Mysterious Forces dominate social phenomena and processes. In war and armed struggle, this feature of social processes is brought to its peak. Here everything seems unclear, mystical, unreasonable, anti-human. In other areas, alienation also finds expression in the creation of contradictions between man and the products of his Labor. In war, things created by man become means for his physical destruction. In this sense, we can say that the specific Essence of wars is closer to mysticism than those antinomies and contradictions of nature that epistemologically gave rise to Kant's agnostic doctrine of "impenetrable noumena."

The objective nature of wars is a more powerful source of mysticism and agnosticism than all other social and natural phenomena.

And now, when the nuclear abyss of non-existence is revealed before history, it is quite natural to expect that "the Enlightenment will completely abandon its children" and give preference to some modern, modernized forms of irrationalism, both in the scientific explanations of the contemporary acute and super-acute contradictions in the military sphere, and especially in the aggression against the ordinary consciousness of the masses of the people. (See: and Yasukov. M. I. Philosophical Problems of War and Peace. Knowledge. 1984. Page 37.).

In methodological terms, Marxist epistemology most resolutely rejects all old and new attempts of agnosticism and irrationalism to nestle in the doctrine of the nature, essence and character of wars, and also in the scientific problems of military science in particular. Despite their undoubted specificity, war and armed struggle are objectively presupposed social phenomena, existing and developing according to their own laws. They are as knowable as any other natural or social phenomenon. Their cognition is nothing but a reflective, not an irrational process.

Significant changes also occurred in the methodological requirement of Marxist-Leninist epistemology for the unity of the sensory and logical in military cognitive and military scientific activity. The path of knowledge of military phenomena also begins with living contemplation, then passes to abstract thinking, and ends in human practice, as Vladimir Ilyich Lenin taught. However, in this dialectic of the sensory and logical in the military cognitive process, a number of peculiarities are manifested.

Above all, the role of implementation is constantly growing, such as abstraction, analysis, synthesis, generalization, modeling, and others.

This feature contains an additional danger of sensory blindness, which is a violation of the unity of logical knowledge with the sensory. In addition, the very nature of the sensory in wars and armed struggle, the fact that here the energy of external irritation becomes an immediate danger to the life of the knowing subject, also strengthens and sharpens the contradictions of the sensory with the logical, and is able to divert the latter from the truth. In the same direction, in the conditions of armed struggle, the possibility of an overwhelming density of sensory data or, conversely, the scarcity characteristic of the same data will act, which in no way relieves the commander from the obligation to make decisions. With the availability of modern and ultra-modern means of intelligence, the dependence of the cognitive process on deliberate disinformation will manifest itself with even greater force than in the past, which is also capable of disrupting the unity of the sensory and logical in the cognitive process, of diverting it in the direction of false facts or false assumptions, assessments and conclusions.

These features of the military cognitive process express its contradictory nature, and with greater force require corresponding dialectical thinking on the part of the command staff. This is actually the main complex methodological requirement, in which all the dialectical features of the cognitive process in the conditions of armed struggle are synthesized. The same requirement arises from the dialectical-materialist theory of truth, with the difference that here other opposites and contradictions come to the fore, in which objective knowledge, the objectivity of truth, interact with the subjective aspirations, desires, goals of the belligerents, and absolute knowledge with the relative, changing theoretical positions of military science and abstract definitions with the concreteness of their application in accordance with the changing conditions of war activity. The specificity of the processes of war, and armed struggle, emphasizes with great force the need to combine strict objectivity with a creative attitude to the cognitive and practical problems of combat activity.

This is also a complex methodological requirement with a primary role in the training of the military cadres of the socialist army, and also the way in which socialist military science develops its contemporary private scientific issues.

In the light of the dialectical-materialist theory of truth and its characteristic features and peculiarities of manifestation in military affairs, the complete unsuitability and dangerous consequences of manifestations of subjectivism and degraded activity, of relativism and dogmatism, of an abstract, non-concrete approach detached from real military phenomena and processes, which also takes the form of a dogmatic attitude to the dialectics of one or another truth, with the conditions of its practical use as a means, stand out with greater force.

In modern conditions, the methodological role of those requirements that arise from the Marxist-Leninist doctrine of the essence and role of social practice in the process of knowledge has also grown extremely much. In principle, its military modification, which is military policy, but taken in inseparable unity with social practice in the broad sense of the word, is the basis and goal of military knowledge and the criterion of truth. But in this principle there are very significant features that introduce additional moments into the requirements themselves.

In this connection, one cannot fail to note the increased contradiction between the goals that military science seeks to substantiate and the enormous capabilities of modern weapons to turn into Absurdity and victory, as a global goal of war. It is from this contradiction that strong hesitations arose regarding the political Essence of missile-nuclear war, and ultimately this connection was severed.

The most serious attention deserves the way in which military practice fulfills its functions as a criterion for truth. In principle, Lenin's formulation of the dialectic of the definiteness and indefiniteness of practice retains its force here, which allows this formulation to be a reliable criterion of truth and at the same time to reveal sufficient scope for its continuous creative development. In modern warfare, however, the indefiniteness of military practice has greatly increased, insofar as its true state in the face of armed struggle cannot be recreated in the practice of peacetime training of troops. This circumstance also introduces greater indefiniteness into the payments for waging modern War and requires from socialist Military Science a freer, more flexible and more variant solution of those questions of war activity that cannot be practically verified in peacetime conditions. The role of modeling various aspects of combat activity has grown and is growing to a great extent.

If we take military practice in a synthetic form in its relation to the synthetic form of contemporary knowledge of military phenomena, we could note the action of several new trends in their mutual dialectical development.

First, in socio-political terms, the state of military practice when it collapses as a systematized human material activity is still underestimated. In this state, the practice coincides with the final results of nuclear war and ceases to perform any functions.

Nuclear weapons have a socio-political form, but they are born entirely from the transforming material power of the atomically armed man, and it is precisely this state of the entire sensory material activity that must be studied by modern science, including military science, with absolute precision and without any detours or economies.

Secondly, there are great objective possibilities that this issue will end up in the same state on a purely military level. For example, when the use of nuclear munitions for defensive purposes or for offensive purposes is envisaged for the conduct of a battle or operation on limited areas, without taking into account the real consequences of such combat activity. Perhaps in this case we are faced with the deception of abstraction, when it has not yet been supported and verified in real practical activity. Another thing would happen if two belligerents actually inflicted on each other on a limited section of the front as many nuclear and other strikes as are now inflicted in the minds of the staff exercises. Only then, on the basis of this already real criterion, can the truths necessary for military science be discovered. But this is impossible, which is why something else remains in force, namely, with severely limited possibilities for military practice to fulfill its functions in relation to military science.

Thirdly, since ancient times, military practice has been divided into peacetime and wartime, between which a sensitive difference always remains, no matter how close the peacetime training of troops is to combat activity. In the conditions of using weapons of mass destruction, this difference will undergo qualitative changes. It is not excluded that combat activity will appear outside the control of what was typical for peacetime practical training of troops.

Fourth, the uncertainty and relativity of the target connections and dependencies between the troops, as a practice and as a military science, is growing incredibly. Not only at the planetary level, within the framework of the World Nuclear War, but also at all lower Levels of combat activity, national, regional front, district, sector and others, with which the military is now accustomed to handling, 100 times more powerful material factors will appear, counteracting the successful implementation of combat goals and tasks. All this is another evidence in favor of Friedrich Engels' thesis about the inevitable demise of militarism... As a result of its own development, including on the battlefield, and not only when it destroys the peaceful centers of the belligerents, and the common Home of all peoples - planet Earth.

FOR THE AUTHOR.

Professor, Doctor of Philosophy, Colonel, Dimitar Petrov Bantutov passed away in 2019. The man Dimitar Petrov Bantutov lived with dignity and served the Motherland honestly.

Here is what the man Dimitar Bantutov wrote in 1986:

"But even dogmatism (in socialism) must reconsider some of its views:

For example, the hope that the demise of capitalism is a matter of the foreseeable historical future, or that capitalism has exhausted all its possibilities for the development of productive forces, or the view of the absolute unsuitability of the economic system of capitalism, and the impossibility of its being reformed in a democratic direction, or the possibilities of bourgeois democracy developing in some countries, in a very wide range of democracy, which creates great, still poorly studied and poorly used, peaceful possibilities for the progress of humanity.

In 1986, Colonel, Professor Bantutov taught philosophy at the G.S. Rakovski Military Academy. He held the position of deputy head of the philosophy department. Then Dimitar Bantutov wrote the book "Imperatives of Time". The main idea of the book is that socialism cannot win victory over capitalism through the use of nuclear weapons. The reason is that after a nuclear war, both capitalism and socialism will not exist. The human race will not exist. This idea was in sharp contradiction with the "revolutionary ideas" of dogmatic left-wing socialism. In totalitarian societies, such ideas are pursued:

Colonel Bantutov was disciplinary dismissed from the G.S. Rakovski Military Academy, was expelled from the ranks of the Bulgarian Communist Party, a procedure for dismissal and revocation of the rank of colonel was initiated, and Dimitar Bantutov had to be tried by a military court.

Colonel Bantutov was not tried by a military court. The reason is that Dimitar Bantutov was playing tennis on the court, together with the then Minister of Defense, Army General Dobri Dzhurov. The general terminated the court proceedings. The general saved the colonel.

According to the words of the first democratically elected president of Bulgaria, Zhelyu Zhelev, Dimitar Bantutov is the only senior political officer who was actually repressed by the totalitarian regime in Bulgaria.

The book "Imperatives of Time. Theory of War and Peace," was published in 1990.